THE GENEROSITY GENE

Discovering Your Spiritual DNA

by Brian Campbell

Made For More Publishing, madeformore.io
Editing by David Moore II
Copyediting by Jill M. Smith
Book Cover by Rigel-Drake Garcia

ISBN 978-0-9896919-9-4 (Softcover)
ISBN 978-0-9896919-8-7 (Hardcover)

Library of Congress Control Number 2022944774
10 9 8 7 6 5 4 3 2 1
1st Edition, August 2022

Printed in the United States of America

DEDICATION

To Jamie, my best friend, love of my life, ministry partner, and wife of forty-plus years. What a journey we have shared together. Thank you for your tremendous personal sacrifice, constant encouragement, brilliant insights, and tireless editing. We have a story to tell! It's one of personal generosity that began in extreme humility and lack. But we still found ways to be generous with our time and talent. As the Lord began to bless our life financially, we made giving to missions our priority. Scripture states that "two shall become one." Our life's journey has been a singular one. My hope and prayer are that our example and story might inspire others toward a life of generosity. I love you, Campbell!

ENDORSEMENTS

Through the many years that we have known Brian, one fact has never been in doubt—his and his family's commitment to being generous people. He is thus well suited to make a major literary contribution to the subject. This book is well written, well researched and rich in thought and content. We highly commend it.

Paul Alexander, PhD and Carol Alexander, PhD
President and Dean of the Graduate School
Trinity Bible College and Graduate School, Ellendale, ND
TrinityBibleCollege.edu

They say when reading a book one should read the author. My wife Kathy and I have "read" Brian's and Jamie Campbell's lives for many years. They are authentic givers in all their talent, time, and treasure. The Generosity Gene is a powerful reflection of their spiritual DNA, truly practicing what they preach. Your generosity horizon will expand to the big picture as you read. It's a winner.

Jim Cantelon
Founder/President
WOW Working for Orphans & Widows
WowMissionUSA.com

Brian not only teaches about generosity, he practices it. Embedded in each of us is the ability to be generous because we were created in the image of God. Brian combines biblical principles with personal experiences that will help you grow your generosity into its intended purposes.

Doug Clay
General Superintendent
Assemblies of God USA
AG.org

Brian takes us on a fascinating generosity journey, which blends his own personal examples with biblical precepts. Read it, soak it in, and allow it to change your life!

Dr. Marek Kaminski
Bishop
Pentecostal Church in Poland

It is with great respect that I share my endorsement of Brian's message through this powerful concept of the generosity gene. Having partnered with Brian in missions and global outreach on several occasions, both in the U.S. and in Italy, I can personally attest to the fact that he has practiced his procedures with excellence and generosity, and because of that, nations have been impacted! As a friend and fellow Buckeye and golfing friend to my late husband, Rick Pasquale, Brian and his wife Jamie were instrumental in sowing seeds of faith into our missions efforts in Europe! Thank you, Brian! I will use this teaching in many ministry opportunities in Italy and beyond!

Pastor Jennifer J. Pasquale
Lead Pastor
ICF Rome, Italy
ICFRome.org

For over ten years, we have witnessed Brian and Jamie first-hand, as they have lived out a huge heart for God's kingdom through generosity! This book is WHO THEY ARE! Their journey has inspired us to take larger steps of faith and believe God for miraculous experiences. Brian and Jamie are a testimony to God's provision and faithfulness. If you long to grow in your stewardship and kingdom impact, this book is for you! Allow it to touch your life, and then pass it on to others who want their lives to make a BIG impact!

Pastor Darin and Jayne Poli
Executive Pastor
Emmanuel Christian Center
EmmanuelCC.org

The Generosity Gene details the journey of Brian and Jamie Campbell and their trust in God's character and provision through seasons of highs and lows. Brian Campbell illustrates through Scripture the generous nature of God and the need for believers made in His image to reflect that generosity in their lives and their community. While the premise of the book is to awaken this generosity gene in our spiritual DNA, it is also a reminder of the goodness and faithfulness of God, who can be trusted in all things, including your finances.

Rev. Dan Holmes and Rev. Dr. Stephanie C. Holmes
Founders
Autism Spectrum Resources for Marriage & Family
HolmesASR.com

Brian has been a friend for over forty years. We were intrigued by this insightful take on Christ living generously through us. *The Generosity Gene* is a fresh reminder that the DNA of Jesus is in us! This is a must-read that will bring a biblical and balanced view of giving to any follower of Jesus.

Pastor John and Diane Baschieri
Lead Pastor
New Life Church, Lehigh Acres, FL
NewLifeLehigh.com

The Generosity Gene is recommended for anyone who wants to experience growth in their spiritual journey. Brian does an excellent job writing the case for the "generosity gene." He said so well that when you grasp your spiritual identity, it will change the course of your spiritual journey. You will be reminded of how God's grace and generosity are inseparable toward us. I have known Brian Campbell for several years, and he is a man of his word. He lives out what he preaches and has seen the faithful hand of God powerfully move in his life! This book is filled with nuggets of truth, which will encourage you to take your faith to the next level.

Pastor Rusty Railey
Lead Pastor
JFA Church, Joliet, IL
JFA.church

My friend Brian Campbell has written a book for everyone who desires the blessings that accompany a generous life and an eternity of great reward. *The Generosity Gene* will draw you in as you read the personal experiences and "God moments" of Brian and Jamie's generosity journey. No doubt a book for every pastor and follower of Jesus!

Pastor Dave Divine
Lead Pastor
Chapelhill Church, Douglasville, GA
ChapelHill.cc

Within the pages of Brian's book, *The Generosity Gene*, you will find nuggets of truth, principles of faith, and, most importantly, practices that are Spirit inspired and biblically profound. Each chapter walks you through the opportunity to supernaturally discover and develop the resources to draw people into these powerful truths. You will enjoy each chapter, and you may need to find an extra highlighter. Thanks, Brian, for sharing part of your journey with us.

Rick Allen
National Light for the Lost Director
Assemblies of God
LFTL.ag.org

As we see inflation plaguing country after country, governments falling, chaos reigning, and a large number of other calamities raging indiscriminately across our world, it has caused many to embrace a fearful, self-preserving, and selfish outlook. In the midst of all this, it is refreshing to see *The Generosity Gene*, an uplifting book that shares biblical wisdom and great stories of faith and transparency. It is imperative during this difficult time that all Christians rise up in generosity with their talent, time, and money. Brian has given us a book that will inspire and increase faith in all of us to do more than we could ever imagine as we learn the greater joy of generosity. A great read that will edify, encourage, and change the reader forever.

Pastor Dishan Wickramaratne
Lead Pastor   *Former General Superintendent*
People's Church, Sri Lanka   Assemblies of God, Sri Lanka
PeoplesChurch.lk

Brian Campbell loves life, loves people, and loves the gospel of Jesus Christ. For him, kingdom generosity is all about the story of Jesus being spread to every corner of the Earth. *The Generosity Gene* can serve as a compass for all who desire to better put their treasure where their heart is and are willing to embark on an incredible journey of faith! We heartily recommend *The Generosity Gene* to you and all you serve.

Randy and Becky Young
Founders and Directors
The Agora Group
TheAgoraGroup.org

Nothing inspires us like a great story. Brian's stories of big faith and radical obedience will inspire you to take God at His Word. The practical application of timeless spiritual principles accompanied by examples of divine intervention will both challenge and encourage every reader to unlock their own generosity gene!

Pastor Adam Detamore
Lead Pastor
Real Life Church, Greenfield, IN
ReaLifeChurch.org

Christianity has always been and will forever be a movement of generosity, thanks in part to individuals like Brian Campbell, who not only lives it out but also writes it out. This is one of those books that carries the movement forward.

Pastor CJ Johnson
Senior Pastor
Northview Church, Carmel, IN
NorthViewChurch.us

Out of our relationship that spans decades, we have seen Brian and Jamie Campbell live the principles shared in this book. It is one thing to talk about generosity but another to walk it out. You will be encouraged, inspired, and challenged as Brian shares his heart with authenticity. Lean in and open your heart. The principles in this book have the potential to change your life.

Ed and Christy Ivie
CEO and Founders
exo18
exo18.com

Generosity is the ability to place value on others and discover your true purpose for living. *The Generosity Gene* is not just a book but a vehicle for success.

Bishop Rick Thomas
Senior Pastor
Abundant Life Church, Margate, FL
AbundantLife.tv

The Generosity Gene is a gift to the Body of Christ in challenging times. Campbell mines the deep truths of Scripture and marries them to his personal journey of faith, sacrifice, missional focus, and expectation that God sees and rewards! If there was ever a time when the church needs to hear this message of generosity, it is now!

Jeff Dove
Director
Life Publishers International
FireBible.com

Brian Campbell embodies the essence of *The Generosity Gene*. This book will unpack the transferable principles of generosity that lead to a life and ministry of exponential return.

Pastor Aaron Cole
Lead Pastor
Life Church, Germantown, WI
LifeChurchWI.com

Brian Campbell takes the reader on a personal journey of faith. Read this thought-provoking book with expectation as he provides practical steps to releasing extravagant generosity. *The Generosity Gene* is not only a must read, but it will become a lifestyle for those desiring to live in next-level generosity.

Pastor Mark English
Lead Pastor
CLC Church, Bensalem, PA
CLCOnline.org

Brian encapsulates his life mission to inspire generosity through personal testimonies and faith-filled principles in *The Generosity Gene*. His unique blend of practical teaching and God-inspired moments of his personal journey will motivate every reader to take responsibility for what they can do and live open-handedly.

Larry Henderson
Europe Regional Director
Assemblies of God World Missions
EuropeMissions.org

CONTENTS

FOREWORD

Brian and I met almost twenty years ago. Our journey has taken us around the world, speaking and teaching together on four continents. When you travel with someone, you get to know them well, quickly. Sitting next to each other on a plane for twelve hours at a time, our conversations built mutual understanding and depth of connection that mere acquaintances never reach.

Brian's years of faith and generosity have given him the opportunity and experience to tackle this subject as an expert. People can argue with your doctrine or denomination affiliation, but it's much harder to deny the fact that your life has been changed. The testimony found in this book is proof that you cannot outgive God.

My friend Dick Foth says, "We teach what we know, but we reproduce who we are." Brian has not only reproduced this life of "radical generosity" in his biological children, he has also multiplied himself through the thousands of people he has invested in throughout his thirty-plus years of ministry.

Brian considers my dad his spiritual father. Dad built my spiritual foundation as well. For as long as I can remember he taught us that "if God can get it through you, He'll give it to you." This DNA is evident in Brian's life.

The Generosity Gene is a must-read. I'm convinced generosity is the most attractive quality an individual can possess. It is the heart of God the Father. "For God so LOVED the world that He GAVE . . ." You can give without loving, but you cannot love without giving. Love and generosity are who God is and who He desires us to be. Dig into this book, open your heart, and start living a life of radical generosity. It's in your genes. It will transform you into your best possible you.

Brad Rosenberg
Chief Partnership Officer
Convoy of Hope
brosenberg@convoyofhope.org

INTRODUCTION

"I can tell you from personal experience, there is no greater adventure on Earth than simply living the life of generosity available to all God's people—but that so few ever dare to live."
Robert Morris

"Life is a journey, not a destination."
Ralph Waldo Emerson

"Skills, talent, and experience are all important, but the generosity gene creates the foundation for great leadership. I have never seen a great leader that didn't have the generosity gene."
Jack Welch

For many years, I have known that I had a book on generosity incubating and marinating inside me. Along the way, there have been a few attempts to complete it. But with each attempt, I simply knew it was not ready. To be candid, I simply was not ready! Then an opportunity presented itself to pursue a master's degree in missional leadership at Trinity Graduate School. As much as I love missions and am always looking to hone my leadership skills, I knew the main takeaway for the master's program was to prep for this book. At almost sixty years of age, I would find it to be one of the most challenging undertakings of my adult life, but also one of the most rewarding.

During my thesis research on generosity, titled *Inspiring Generosity: An Inter-Generational Perspective*, I came across a significant quote by Jack Welch: "Skills, talent, and experience are important, but **the generosity gene** creates the foundation for great leadership."[1] Some time later, I came across another one from him: "I have never seen a great leader that didn't have **the generosity gene**."[2] I became quite enamored with the idea of an actual generosity gene. As you will see, I am absolutely convinced that not only does such a gene exist but that it also resides in everyone. It is my hope that after you finish reading this book, you will arrive at the same conclusion.

As a young man, I bought into the idea that life is all about the journey and not a destination at which to arrive this side of heaven. Heaven, of course, is the destination goal! Simply stated, *The Generosity Gene* is a compilation of our life's journey and the many key principles and insights we have learned along the way. In addition, I will unpack the idea that each of us has been equipped with a God-given "generosity gene" along with all the resources we need for our generosity journey. In forty-plus years of marriage and ministry, Jamie and I have shared an amazing journey. We have a story to tell. It is one that depicts a life built upon a scriptural foundation, biblical precepts, and real-life experience. We can look back now and see that even in the early,

---

1 Jeff Haden, "Jack Welch Reveals the 1 Quality Every Great Leader Possesses," Inc.com (New York), July 6, 2006.

2 "Want to Get Promoted? Jack Welch Describes the Most Important Trait You Need," linkedin.com, July 21, 2016 https://www.linkedin.com/pulse/want–get–promoted–jack–welch–describes–most–important–jeff–haden/

formative stages of our marriage, God was fashioning a unique path for our life together—a path that would become paramount to our journey. As a young married couple still in Bible college and simply trying to make ends meet, the early stages of our journey were incredibly humble. And yet God was laying a solid foundation for our life's journey into fully embracing the spiritual and practical dynamics of generosity.

Our generosity journey has been impacted significantly by others who have adamantly pursued their own. Throughout this book, I will share some of their insights and stories as to how they inspired Jamie and me to press forward in our own journey. Our sincere hope is that some of our stories and insights will do the same for you, the reader—to inspire you to greater generosity. Robert Morris, author of *The Blessed Life*, speaks to the sober reality that the generosity lane is a road less traveled: "I can tell you from personal experience, there is no greater adventure on Earth than simply living the life of generosity and abundance that is available to all of God's people—but that so few ever dare to live."[3] Sadly, it took thirty years of pastoral experience to reinforce the Robert Morris narrative to myself that so few dare to pursue a life of generosity. I found a similar statement in the book *Contagious Generosity: Creating a Culture of Giving in Your Church*, where the authors quote Walter B. Russell: "The road to generosity is a journey that few Christians successfully

---

3 Robert Morris, *The Blessed Life: The Simple Secret of Achieving Guaranteed Financial Results* (Ventura: Regal Books, 2002), 15.

complete."[4] As you know, any journey is taken one step at a time. You will see that I take the one-step-at-a-time approach in my writing. My real passion is to help inspire you to move forward in a positive direction in your own generosity journey as you discover and activate the generosity gene within.

I have always believed one of the most powerful communication tools is story. During my research, I was surprised to find that there was actual scientific evidence to support my belief. Dr. Paul Zak is a leading researcher on the biological effects that story has on the human brain. Zak discovered that the brain releases the neurochemical oxytocin when stimulated by a compelling story. It is this neurochemical that can move people to be kind, compassionate, and generous. Zak's states that "oxytocin makes people want to help others in costly and tangible ways."[5] All because of a story.

In short, we have been designed biologically by our Creator to be responsive, in the moment, to a story that touches both our intellect and our emotions. It could be argued that Jesus was the greatest storyteller of all time. He provided us with the greatest message and the greatest method to communicate the message. In fact, Jesus used story at least 118 times in the Gospels to communicate His message. My life has been impacted dramatically by the examples and stories of others.

---

4 Chris Willard and Jim Sheppard, *Contagious Generosity: Creating a Culture of Giving in Your Church* (Grand Rapid: Zondervan, 2012).
5 Paul J. Zak, "Why Inspiring Stories Make Us React: The Neuroscience of Narrative," Cerebrum 2, no. 2 (February2015):2, https://www.ncbi.nlm.nih.gov/pmc/articles/PMC4445577.

My hope is that you, the reader, will be inspired and impacted by some of the stories in our generosity journey. In fact, just to prep you, you may very well experience what I like to refer to as "God moments." I develop the concept of God moments in chapter two but encourage you to be open to the Holy Spirit's promptings in your heart as you read.

I passionately believe that the activated and unleashed generosity gene in you has transformational capabilities. Author Barbara Bonner states, "Generosity is an activity that can change the world. . . . Generosity can transform our place in the world and how we live our lives. Generosity can be revolutionary."[6] My prayer is that this book will be informational, inspirational, but most of all, transformational in your heart and life.

On a final introductory note, I sense a tremendous obligation to reach emerging generations—in particular, Millennials and Gen Z-ers. By no means am I an expert or authority on what might be meaningful to these precious young minds. In some way, shape, or form, I want to pass the baton of generational generosity to them. I honestly and personally know of no other way to do so than to offer our generosity journey as an example of what can happen when generosity is modeled in a radical way. It is my belief that God has a divine generosity design for each of us. Many times, we may need a boost of encouragement along the way to be generous at new levels. As a young pastor, I had a

6 Barbara Bonner, *Inspiring Generosity* (Somerville: Wisdom Publications, 2014), 1.

very wise pastor, Charles Cookman, offer these words to me as he was nearing retirement: "Brian, faith never gets any easier." This statement has served us well through the years and helped us each time we sensed God moving us to a new level of generosity.

Friends, it's true: Faith never gets any easier. Recently, my good friend and pastor, Dave Divine, made this statement: "It requires faith to experience God-sized dreams, and it usually requires risk." As you read, I trust you will find moments of renewed faith and courage to face the risks involved in moving to new levels in your own generosity journey!

CHAPTER 1 THE FOUNDATION

"Generosity is, at heart, a response to the gift of God's grace through Jesus Christ."
Chris Willard and Jim Sheppard

There is an introductory phrase I like to use when I am speaking somewhere for the first time: You see the glory, but you may not know the story. I then share that if you were to take a snapshot of our life over the past forty-plus years of marriage, ministry, and family, you would say that the Campbells have been tremendously blessed. And you would be correct. In other words, you would "see the glory." This is a precursor to me sharing some or many aspects of our generosity journey with God's coinciding favor and blessing. Typically, I would share our story in a chronological manner. But, for the purposes of this book, I'll begin with the most recent and possibly the most dramatic part of our generosity journey. I will go into greater detail later in the book, but for now, here is an excerpt from a message I preached, titled "What Could God Do with the Stuff of Our Lives?"

> In late 2016, the Lord would surprise us again with
> our most significant "epiphany" to date. Jamie and
> I came to a very clear "revelation knowing" that,
> after thirty years of lead pastor ministry, we were
> finished pastoring, and He had a new assignment

for us. God was calling us out of pastoral ministry and into a hybrid mission's role as a "Missions Ambassador." God wanted us to start traveling and share our stories of generosity. So in July 2017, we launched BJC Missions. We took a 40 percent pay cut with no benefits! For eighteen years, the Lord had asked for our savings, and along the way He has asked for some of our "stuff." But in 2016, He asked for the rest of our lives! So we launched out into the deep, and here we are. No regrets! Because we truly believe that the most important day of the harvest is the day you choose your seed, and only God can count all the apples in a seed.

Every story, every journey has a starting point or a beginning. We believe your individual starting point is the foundation of *your* journey. A journey of generosity!

Your generosity journey will mirror your spiritual journey.

A solid spiritual formation or foundation was not established for me until my late teen years. My parents divorced when I was eleven years old. Up to that point, I had attended either parochial schools or catechism classes, where I learned about God but was never introduced to a personal relationship with Him. My five siblings and I were raised by hard-working parents who loved us and provided well for us. My earliest observations of generosity were modeled by both of them. However, the fallout of divorce would take its toll on my siblings and me and resulted in the six of us being split between our parents' homes and never living under the same roof again.

By fourteen years of age, I began to find solace in smoking marijuana and dabbling with various pharmaceuticals that were provided by my best friend. He had confiscated them from his grandmother's vast supply. For the next three years, the experimentation would progress to daily use and low-level dealing. Even though I was a stand-out baseball player in high school, I decided to quit sports, and during my junior year, I quit school altogether. This would result in my life taking an epic downhill slide that was getting out of control. I was rapidly heading toward addiction, jail or prison time, and self-destruction. But I had a praying mom!

After the divorce, my mother was hospitalized as a result of an emotional breakdown. While in the hospital, she was visited by her brother, my Uncle Charlie, who led her to the Lord. God healed her and dramatically changed her life. As a result, she immediately began praying for her six kids. I am happy to report that her prayers were answered, and we have all come to have a personal relationship with Jesus.

For me, it happened on August 20, 1976, while visiting my oldest brother, Dave, in Dickinson, Texas. I would soon realize that Dave and my sister Debbie had also been praying for me, and they were instrumental in talking me into that life-changing trip to Texas. While sitting in my brother's living room, I experienced the presence of the Holy Spirit in a tangible way. For years, the only emotion I seemed to be capable of was anger, but in a matter of moments, the Holy Spirit touched and melted my hardened heart. On that fateful summer day, my spiritual foundation was established. I began as a complete blank slate. Up to that point, I had no memory of ever reading the Bible and wasn't familiar with anything most kids learn in children's church. My life was now secure on a sure foundation, but I simply knew nothing of what that meant. During the early stages of my spiritual formation, I experienced the tremendous grace of God and began to grasp His bountiful and incredible generosity toward me.

Where Does Generosity Come From?

If I were to summarize *The Generosity Gene* into one thought, it would be to encourage growth in your spiritual journey and to make sure that journey is established on a solid foundation. I am convinced that understanding and experiencing God's grace in a personal and tangible way is paramount to establishing such a solid foundation. The authors of *Contagious Generosity*, Chris Willard and Jim Sheppard, describe it best: "Generosity is at its core a lifestyle, a lifestyle in which we share all that we have, are, and ever will become as a demonstration of God's love and a response to God's grace."[7] They go on to say that we can't accept God's grace and *not* practice generosity. The two cannot be

---

7 Willard and Sheppard, *Contagious Generosity,* 18.

separated. At the risk of sounding cliché, suffice it to say I believe that your generosity journey will mirror your spiritual journey.

While doing research for my master's thesis, I did a deep dive into the origins of generosity. Based upon your psychology or theology, the origin of generosity is either founded in God or in man. I give place for this discussion because I would be remiss to assume everyone who reads this book believes in either creationism or authentic spiritual formation. Rather, some would take a psychological or humanistic view as to the origins of generosity. Respectfully, I would like to share some of my research findings.

First, let us take a brief look at generosity from a psychological vantage point. The psychology of generosity begins and ends its findings and analysis with the study of humans. Professor Aafke Komter suggests that "the origins of generosity are explored by combining biological, psychological, anthropological, and sociological evidence."[8] These would also be the core values and basis for an evolutionary framework. Further, psychologists would argue that there is no generosity gene. David King, an assistant professor from Indiana University, states, "Of course, there's no gene for generosity. We are not born generous, but it is a way of life in which we have been formed. Generosity is a habit,

---

8 Aafke Komter, "The Evolutionary Origins of Human Generosity," International Sociology 25, no. 3 (2010):443, https://doi.org/10.1177/0268580909360301.

but it [is] also a practice. ... It is looking to practice generosity in whatever we are doing that forms a generous life."[9]

If this happens to be your preferred opinion, you have chosen a journey based upon a foundation that begins and ends with humanity. I would ask you to continue reading as we look at generosity from a theological or spiritual perspective. It is an eternal perspective that begins with the Creator of the heavens and earth, whose kingdom is everlasting!

God's plan is to make His grace—His generosity— personal to each of us.

If there is indeed a generosity gene—and I am convinced there is—it must have an origin in God. My goal is to not lose your interest in mounds of theological rhetoric. Rather, allow me to simply list several biblical truths reinforced by research. This will help establish a solid spiritual understanding as a basis for one's generosity journey:

> "For this is how God loved the world: He **gave** his one and only Son, so that everyone who believes in him will not perish but have eternal life" (John 3:16).
>
> In his book *Radical Charity: How Generosity Can Save the World (And the Church)*, Christopher Marlin-Warfield says, "Generosity is a defining aspect of

---

9 David P. King, "Millennials, Faith and Philanthropy: Who Will be Transformed?" Bridge/Work 1, no. 2 (Spring 2016): 9, http://scholar.valpo.edu/ilasbw/vol1/iss1/2.

CHAPTER 1   THE FOUNDATION

God's character and is baked into the moral structure of the universe . . . . If we understand that Jesus is our clearest image of God and that God's character is reflected in the nature of the universe, then we have reason to believe that the cosmic order is fundamentally generous . . . . In the opening chapter of Genesis—and throughout the Bible—those authors are telling us that God is generous, and that God's generosity is embedded in the universe."[10]

"So God created human beings in his own image. In the image of God he created them; male and female he created them" (Gen. 1:27).

We all have been created in the image of God, and we are called His sons and daughters. Therefore, we absolutely, unequivocally possess the generosity gene in our spiritual DNA through Jesus Christ! In essence, God's grace through Jesus is His greatest act of generosity. When we accept God's grace of generosity through Jesus, the generosity gene is ready for activation in our lives. God's grace and generosity are inseparable. His plan is to make His grace—His generosity—personal to each of us. This is the key to our own unique generosity journey.

God's Generosity Toward Me

Like you, my early experiences into God's grace and goodness far outdistanced my understanding and comprehension of it. Soon after coming to Christ, I was fortunate to get connected to

---

10 Christopher Marlin–Warfield, *Radical Charity: How Generosity Can Save the World (And the Church)* (Eugene: Cascade Books, 2019), 67–69.

a dynamic youth pastor, Terry Hoggard, who nurtured me in all things spiritual. He also offered a friendship that would be vital to me as I began to break the ties to my past. I had only been saved about six months when the lead pastor's wife shared with me that God had a call on my life for ministry. Honestly, I was shocked! I had no qualifications, experience, knowledge, and so on. In my mind, I was still a babe in Christ. But things started to accelerate over the next year as Terry, along with a few other adult youth leaders, recognized my leadership gift and began to cultivate it.

Before God asks anything of you, He first demonstrates it.

As I began considering my college options, several things became clear: (1) I had no resources for college; (2) I didn't want to go to a Bible college as I was still wrestling with the call of God on my life; and (3) I was struggling with fear and insecurities. Although I did go back to high school and graduate, my inner-city school offered a subpar education, so I was probably at a ninth-grade education level. I had never written a term paper, given a speech, or taken any courses beyond the basics. I wasn't ready for college. But, despite my shortcomings, God was ready for me to get on with His plan for me. I was offered a partial baseball scholarship to Evangel University in Springfield, Missouri, but I still had my own costs. Unfortunately, due to a broken finger that required surgery, I was unable to work and earn money, so I did not have the twenty-five-dollar application fee. Yep, I was that poor! I obviously needed a miracle of provision.

One evening I put on headphones and turned on worship music. I began to pray and simply ask the Lord what to do. I had visited Southeastern Bible College in Lakeland, Florida, but because it was a Bible college, I had ruled it out. Instead, I wanted to go to Evangel, major in Physical Education, and pursue a coaching career. But this particular night, I was ready to submit to whatever God had for me. That was when I experienced a "God moment." A peace came over me, and I had a knowing that I should pursue Southeastern and that the provision was on its way.

The very next morning, there was a knock at the door. A friend of mine had driven his 1973 Camaro Z-28 over to my house. He said, "Brian, last night God spoke to me to give you my car." I stood there in stunned silence as he handed me the keys and title to his beautiful silver sports car, complete with black racing stripes. In that moment, I knew I was supposed to sell the car, as it would pay for most of my first year of school. But I was also experiencing a personal expression of God's generosity toward me. It is important to note that before I ever had any knowledge of the generosity gene within, God was modeling generosity for me in a tangible and personal way.

A second such expression of provision by the Lord happened near the end of my first year at Southeastern. By comparison, it was a much smaller monetary amount but had equal, if not greater, impact on me. The sale-of-the-car money had run out, and I was working part-time. On a particular day, I was broke and needed three dollars to wash my clothes. As I headed to chapel after my first class, I was sulking over having no money—not even enough for laundry. It is quite amazing how quickly we forget God's goodness and provision for us.

Rest in this, you can only be generous because of God's generosity toward you through Jesus.

After chapel, I stopped by the mailroom to check my box, and there was a letter from my youngest sister, Teri. It read, "Dear Brian, I am so embarrassed to send you this, but it's all the money I had. I was sitting in church Sunday and felt the Lord prompt me to send you everything I had in my purse. All I had were these three one-dollar bills." In the middle of the mailroom, I experienced a very humbling God moment. As I stood there with tears running down my face, a few students started to comfort me, as they thought I had just received bad news from home. I couldn't speak. I just thanked them and walked out. That provision of three dollars would have as much impact on my life as the Camaro had. Again, God was making His generosity toward me very personal.

I can look back now and see how those two experiences would serve as important cornerstones in the foundation of my generosity journey. You see, before God asks anything of you, He first demonstrates it. Romans 5:8 states, "But God demonstrates His own love toward us, in that while we were yet sinners, Christ died for us" (NASB95). God will always initiate and demonstrate Himself before He asks anything of you. Your spiritual foundation has nothing to do with anything you have done. It has been completely established in Christ. Rest in this: You can only be generous because of God's generosity toward you through Jesus. Willard and Sheppard put it this way: "Generosity is the fruit of God's grace, the product of a transformed heart, and it develops in an atmosphere that encourages it, celebrates it, and reproduces it over time."[11]

The rest of this book is dedicated to encouraging and celebrating the fruit of God's grace of generosity in you as we build upon the firm foundation you have in Christ. We want to activate and energize your generosity gene and push it to new levels. Hopefully, some of our story and insights will nudge you forward in your journey. You have a significant generosity capacity, and we want to cultivate a desire within you to live it out in a radical way. Wherever you are right now, know that you do possess the generosity gene from God. It's time to grow in it!

---

11 Willard and Sheppard, *Contagious Generosity,* 35.

Chapter 1 Takeaway

Before I build on the foundation I established in this chapter, I want to underscore that God is the most generous person of all time, and He created you with His generosity gene. When I began to grasp my spiritual identity, it changed the course of my spiritual journey. I *wanted* to give of my time, talent, and treasure. Take some time now to ask God to help you grow in that understanding. This is how you begin to activate the generosity gene within you!

Important Note: If you have never begun a spiritual journey founded in Christ, please pause your reading and turn to page 185.

CHAPTER 2 THE GOD MOMENTS

"Whether you turn to the right or to the left, your ears will hear a voice behind you, saying, 'This is the way; walk in it.'"
Isaiah 30:21 NIV

During your generosity journey, you will undoubtedly experience a bevy of what I like to refer to as God moments. These are special occasions when we encounter the tangible presence of the Holy Spirit in our lives. There are multiple terminologies we use to describe God moments: epiphany, revelation, illumination, hearing God's voice audibly or in our "knower," through God's Word, through a prophetic utterance, by gifts of the Spirit; the list goes on. The common denominator is a clear and confirming "knowing" that we are receiving some type of direction, encouragement, inspiration, instruction, and/or calling from the Lord. Many times, these are life-impacting or life-changing experiences. It is my belief that the key to moving forward and maturing spiritually, especially in the arena of generosity, is recognizing and acting upon these special experiences we have with the Holy Spirit.

I experienced two God moments within weeks of each other, in 2018. At first glance, you might question what they have to do with generosity. But let me remind you that God not only reveals His grace and generosity toward us in the early stages of our relationship with Him, He will also grant us special moments along the way to remind us of how much He loves and cares for us.

Ballpark Blessings

If you were to see a snapshot of my man cave, you would quickly recognize that I'm a sports guy. I played baseball through college but have been an avid sports fan my whole life. Jamie has always been a good sport about it (pun intended), and our three daughters were raised to love sports as well. As a hobby, I have been a long-time season ticket holder with the Atlanta Braves. My grandkids Ella, Brody, and Hudson love going to the games, and Easton is about ready to begin his tomahawk chop journey. But in September of 2018, something special occurred.

Once in a while, I will take my grandkids to a game one at a time. This particular night was Hudson's turn. It was a Friday night fireworks game, and I had arranged for us to watch the fireworks from the playing field. It was going to be a late night, so we arrived a little late. As we approached the entry gate, a very tall young man tapped me on the shoulder and said, "My friend and I are in town on business, and we were given some great seats but have an extra pair of tickets. I don't know where your seats might be, but you are welcome to these." He proceeded to hand me the pair of tickets and said, "See ya inside." Well, my humble seats were in the front row of the *upper* deck. I know the stadium map pretty well and recognized that these were four rows off the field, right next to the visitors' dugout—much better than my original seats! When we got to the new seats, Hudson's eyes were as big as saucers. We were literally staring into the visitors' dugout. Wow, what a treat this was going to be!

Between innings, as the players came off the field, one of them would toss a ball into the stands. There were several kids in front of us, and they were able to snag all the balls. Finally, around the fifth inning, Hudson looked up at me and said, "Pop Pop, I really want a ball." My immediate thought was to find a way to get Huds a ball even if it meant jumping in front of one of the young lads to get it. It was at that moment, a God moment, that I knew I was supposed to relax, sit back, and do nothing. What? I'm not going to fabricate this; it wasn't what I wanted to hear. I was determined to get my grandson a ball! However, the check that I felt was so strong that I knew there was more to this moment than what was happening. So I told Hudson to please be patient and that somehow this was going to work itself out.

About the seventh inning, we went for a bathroom break. When we returned to our seats, the guy who gave us the tickets was holding a baseball. He said, "Here ya go, little man. This is for you. I overheard you asking for a ball, and I was able to get it from one of the players." In awe, I thanked him again for his kind and considerate generosity to us as strangers. Immediately, I heard in my knower, "This experience is a metaphor for your faith-generosity journey. I will bring people you have never met into your life to not only supply your needs but also to bless you in unexpected ways." I was seriously fighting back tears of gratitude.

Later, we found out that the seats we were given belonged to Hall of Fame pitcher Tom Glavine. They were his personal seats! The Braves won, we tossed the ball back and forth on the field, and then we watched the fireworks. Oh, what a night!

Business Class Upgrade

A few weeks after the baseball game experience, I was in Zagreb, Croatia, with a group of pastors I was hosting for the incredible launch and dedication of the Croatian *Fire Bible*. It turned out to be a spectacular event, followed by a meal that went late into the night. The plan was to meet in the lobby of the hotel at 6:30 a.m. to begin our trek back to the States. For context, I have had the privilege of traveling to forty-eight different countries and hosting teams all over the world. Needless to say, I am an experienced and savvy traveler. However, I made a very rookie mistake that particular morning. I always shower, pack up, and lay out my travel wear the night before. Typically, I only need twenty minutes or so to be ready to go in the morning. I set my phone alarm for 6:00 a.m. No problem!

The Lord will provide ample reminders of His inseparable grace and generosity toward us along our spiritual generosity journey.

Almost always, especially overseas, I am an early riser, even before my alarm goes off. At 6:35 a.m., I awoke to the room phone ringing. To my horror, I had set my phone alarm for 6:00 p.m. instead of a.m.! I told the team to hop on the airport shuttle, and I would take a taxi straight away. A short time later, I was in a taxi headed for the airport about forty-five minutes away.

Upon arrival, I quickly realized the travel nightmare was about to continue. My passport was nowhere to be found! In my haste to leave the hotel room, I had inadvertently laid it on the counter while collecting my belongings. It would take over an hour for another taxi to bring the passport to me at the airport. In the meantime, I was able to see my travel companions pass through security and passport control. The good news was that this group of pastors was very understanding, and they were all seasoned travelers.

As I circled back to the check-in counter, it was brought to my attention that there was no way I could make my existing flight, and there was only one additional flight available that day. Further, they only had a single seat available but would not let me have it until I had my passport in hand. Essentially, the sequence of events over the next two hours had to be perfect for me to get my passport, secure the last seat available, get processed, and make it to the gate before the door closed.

In a span of three hours, I experienced a whirlwind of emotions. I did not have time to think or process any of them; I only had time to react moment-by-moment, with no clue as to how this was going to unfold. I rushed back to the airline counter, having just retrieved my passport from the taxi driver. I knew things were starting to look up when the agent said, "I forgot to mention that the only seat available is in business class. I will give it to you at no extra cost." Anyone who has ever traveled internationally just let out a big "Amen!" With an upgraded ticket, they offered a preferred line through security. I arrived at the gate just as the boarding process began.

As I sat down in my business-class window seat, the full effect of the previous few hours began to set in. I grabbed my earbuds and turned on some music as we taxied out to the runway. Just as we were taking off, a song by Lauren Daigle, "Everything," began to play. As I listened to the words, I had an emotional God moment:

> When I can't see, You lead me.
> When I can't hear, You show me.
> When I can't stand, You carry me.
> When I'm lost, You find me.
> When I'm weak, You are mighty.
> You are everything I need.

I tried to be discreet as I looked out the window with alligator tears rolling down my face. The Lord brought back to mind the ballgame from a few weeks before. He reminded me that He has already gone before me with every kind of provision that I will need for my journey. The serenity of those moments I will cherish for a lifetime.

Believers are not exempt from battling their humanity.

I believe the Lord will provide ample reminders of His inseparable grace and generosity toward us along our spiritual generosity journey. Again, it bears repeating that God will always show His grace and generosity toward us before He expects anything from us. We receive before we are expected to give. The idea is, "Freely you have received; freely give" (Matt. 10:8 NIV).

God obviously knows how each of us is wired. He also knows that regardless of wiring, human nature is common to all. In our human nature is a propensity toward selfishness. Believers are not exempt from battling their humanity. In fact, the apostle Paul states it clearly: "I affirm, by the boasting in you which I have in Christ Jesus our Lord, I die daily" (1 Cor. 15:31 MEV). In Romans 12:2, Paul instructs, "Do not be conformed to this world, but be transformed by the renewing of your mind, that you may prove what is the good and acceptable and perfect will of God" (MEV).

In other words, if you do not die to your human nature by the renewing of your mind, your tendency will be to yield to the old selfish nature of your humanity. This may sound a bit strange, but please hear me out. On occasion, the reason the Lord may ask for something that challenges your human nature may be to keep your selfish nature under control. Jamie and I have found this to be the case in our lives.

When You're Down to Nothing, God's up to Something

The idea that when we are "down to nothing," God is working behind the scenes became real to me during two specific occasions: one early in my Christian life and another early in our marriage.

You might be familiar with a concept called "faith promise," which many churches use for fundraising. I was first introduced to this concept as a nineteen-year-old college student. I had worked all summer to pay off the balance of my first year but still needed $400 to register for year two. I did not know what I was going to do. As I sat in church on a Sunday morning, my pastor was receiving faith promises for a building program. As he made the appeal, I had a God moment. I sensed I was supposed to faith promise $50 toward the building program. I must admit, I was chuckling inside as I wondered what my insignificant $50 would really accomplish. (I had no idea how formative this would become for my generosity journey and my understanding of the importance of immediate obedience.)

The reason the Lord may ask for something that challenges our human nature may be to keep our selfish nature under control.

So I filled out the faith promise card for $50. The very next day, I received an unexpected check in the mail for $500! I tithed $50 and gave $50 to fulfill my faith promise. I now had my $400 registration miracle in hand. Praise the Lord!

I have a good friend, Jim Cantelon, who leads a world-class missions organization in Canada. One day, we were discussing faith-promise God moments in our lives. He said, "You know, Brian, God moves into the room we create for Him." A faith promise does just that. It creates room for God to move into our lives. I love it!

The second event I want to share was when Jamie and I were living in Manteo, North Carolina, serving in our first full-time position as associate pastors. We had only been there seven months when the lead pastor resigned. This came as a complete shock to us because we were not expecting him to leave so quickly after we came on board.

Around the same time, we were contacted by a church in Charlotte, North Carolina, that was looking for a youth pastor. We were excited for the opportunity. Full of hope and anticipation, we made the almost six-hour drive to Charlotte with our one-year-old daughter, Lindy, in tow. Understand, this was in the days before you could research a place online. When we got there, we immediately loved the lead pastor, Howard Fortenberry, and saw the real potential to grow under his leadership.

Everything was great until he sheepishly brought up the salary. Up to that point in our three-year marriage, we had lived hand to mouth. God always provided, but it was tough sledding at times, especially with a baby to consider. The bottom line is that the salary was less than what we were currently making, and Charlotte had a much higher cost of living. Pastor Fortenberry said, "Even though this is all we can pay, we will take an offering once a month to subsidize your income."

To be completely transparent, our hearts sank. I had really seen this going differently in my mind. They offered us the position on the spot, but we asked for a few days to pray and talk it over.

It was mid-afternoon when we started the drive back to Manteo. After we rode quietly for thirty to forty-five minutes, I looked over at my sweet wife and muttered, "I think the Lord is asking us to come to Charlotte." With tear-filled eyes, she nodded her head in agreement. I knew she was thinking exactly what I was thinking: *How are we going to make ends meet?*

This God moment was one of deep solitude with no fanfare or glitz. It was just a simple, yet profound knowing that "this is the way, walk in it" (Is. 30:21 NIV).

Little could we have known that we would spend the next sixteen years of our lives in ministry at that church. For five years, we served as youth and associate pastors, and when the lead pastor retired, I became the lead pastor. Our other two daughters, Kristy and Keri, were both born in Charlotte. Our daughters' childhoods were spent there. It was there we bought our first home, eventually built a brand-new home, and had many more amazing God moments and some very special generosity stories, which will be shared throughout the pages of this book. But suffice it to say, it was a still, small voice in our hearts during our drive along Interstate 85 all those years ago, that would become foundational to setting the course for our entire ministry.

By no means is this an exhaustive deep dive into the realm of how and when we hear and respond to the tangible presence of God in our lives. Rather, I offer some of our experiences as examples of how the Holy Spirit might appear in your own life. The key is recognizing that God is indeed present and at work in your life, and He wants you to grow and prosper in your walk with Him. A few of the most significant God moments for Jamie and me have been during transitional seasons in our ministry trek.

A Clarion Call

After sixteen years in Charlotte, we had a clarion call that the Lord had another assignment for us. So we resigned our post as lead pastors. However, we literally had no clear direction where to go or what door would open next for us. The board reluctantly accepted our resignation and generously offered us a three-month severance package. Then we simply waited for our next marching orders from on high!

The week before our last Sunday in Charlotte, I bought a Thomas Kincaid screensaver for our desktop Gateway computer. (Ah, the good ole days of large home PC units!) The screensaver contained forty different Kincaid portraits, each with a Scripture verse set to change every two minutes. One afternoon, while passing by the workstation where the computer sat, I noticed the screen slowly transitioning to the next slide. It caught my attention as the verse Isaiah 30:21 appeared: "Whether you turn to the right or to the left, your ears will hear a voice behind you, saying, 'This is the way; walk in it'" (NIV). I stopped in my tracks as the Holy Spirit spoke this word to my heart. I now had a firm word of encouragement that we would have a clear and concise "moment" of knowing that "this is the way; walk in it." The week was so busy leading up to Sunday that I didn't have time to share this word with Jamie. No worries. The Holy Spirit took care of it.

God is indeed present and at work in your life, and He wants you to grow and prosper in your walk with Him.

Sunday came, and even though there was huge emotion and sadness that this chapter of our life was ending, there was also an amazing peace and confidence in our hearts. As I was closing my message, we shared our final goodbyes. Jamie went first. After a few minutes, she concluded her thoughts with the word God had given her. She shared how she was walking by the workstation and saw the screensaver changing pictures. A verse caught her attention. Yep, Isaiah 30:21! I was both gloriously stunned and completely caught off guard as she shared exactly what I was

CHAPTER 2 THE GOD MOMENTS

going to share. All I could do in that moment was echo her words as we both recognized that the Lord had undeniably given us a clear and concise word.

It was only a few days later that I received a call about a church in Hickory, North Carolina. The pastor there had resigned the same Sunday we resigned in Charlotte. We knew nothing of Hickory other than that it was where you went to buy furniture at great prices. We would find out that they had an eleven-person search committee, and one of their core values was that they had to be unanimous in their decision in selecting their next pastor. Somehow, they got our contact information and reached out to me.

All told, the process took about three months. In the final analysis, it came down to two candidates. In the final interviews, they asked us each a single question: "Do you believe God is calling you here to be our lead pastor?" By this time in the process, we knew beyond a shadow of any doubt that this was our next assignment from the Lord. I simply answered, "Yes!" The other candidate could not answer with the same assurance.

The committee spent three days in fasting and prayer before they reconvened on a Wednesday evening. They had come to a unanimous decision, and my phone rang. On the other end was the chairperson of the search committee, and he said these words: "Pastor Brian, we are unanimous in our decision to present you to our congregation as our lead pastor candidate.

Sir, will you accept this invitation?" At that moment, I noticed the screensaver was transitioning. With no exaggeration or embellishment and before I could say a word, the verse appeared on the screen: "Whether you turn to the right or to the left, your ears will hear a voice behind you, saying, 'This is the way; walk in it'" (Is. 30:21 NIV). And we did!

We spent the next eight years of our life and ministry in Hickory. As you will see, we experienced some of our most significant generosity God moments while serving there.

Chapter 2 Takeaway

The God moments in this chapter were included to help you recall your own. I know that just as God has been generous toward me, He has been generous toward you. He is no respecter of persons. Take some time to think about some of the God moments you have had.

CHAPTER 3   THE EXCUSES

"They were being tested by many troubles, and they are very poor. But they are also filled with abundant joy, which has overflowed in rich generosity."
2 Corinthians 8:2

The tithe is a biblical principle. It was and always has been a key part of the foundation of Jamie's and my generosity journey. I will address the tithe in greater detail later in the book, but for now, I will simply reference it as it relates to our story. I recognize that for some the tithe principle may be a brand-new concept. Others may have an alternate view on it altogether. Still others may very well embrace the tithe principle but may struggle to consistently practice it. Please know, whether you are tithing or not, my goal remains the same: to encourage you in your generosity journey. I am believing for you to experience God moments as you read and digest the generosity principles and stories contained within the pages of this book.

I asked Jamie to write the following story, as she was able to recollect the details much better than I was. She is also a very capable communicator in her own right.

Brian and I met at college and married in July of 1980 before his junior year. To say we lived modestly would be an understatement. Brian was a full-time college student and was working part-time to pay his tuition. I worked full-time at a bank, and we lived on my minimum-wage salary. Thankfully, we had plenty of conversations about finances and priorities during our engagement period. During that time, we solidified that the tithe would always be the first check written after payday, and a budget was carefully planned and written out. We were determined to honor God with our finances by being good stewards with our money.

Then came mid-September 1980—six weeks after moving into our government subsidized apartment. We had budgeted $50 for our first electric bill, which seemed like a high but probable amount for the height of summer in Central Florida. When that electric bill arrived, we couldn't believe our eyes—$97! We sat in shock, and then I began to cry. We were unaware of the extra charges included in the first billing cycle. We barely had money for groceries, and now we didn't know what to do with a $47 shortfall.

When we composed ourselves, we knew our commitment to the tithe was being put to the test. So we wrote the tithe check and put it in the church offering the next day. Within hours, we received a call from Brian's mother. (I'd like to interject how blessed we are to have praying mothers!) Through tears, she explained that while in prayer that morning, the Lord impressed on her heart that she was to pay our September car payment. She had no idea why; she just knew that she was supposed to take care of it. Although we would have never asked her to do that, we told her the story of the electric bill. We all had a good cry and marveled at the goodness of God. Oh, and the amount of the car payment? Yep, $47!

Reasons but Not Excuses

It has been my observation from thirty years of pastoring that there are many reasons people get stuck on their spiritual journey. Many times, it can be because of financial duress. If so, the generosity journey can easily get sidetracked, delayed, or worse, completely stuck. Allow me to offer this insight: There is a significant difference between being temporarily paused due to unexpected circumstances and being full-blown stuck. Candidly, stuck people make excuses. Stuck is a very difficult place to be in life, and the longer someone stays stuck, the harder it is to get unstuck.

Disappointment and heartache can ultimately turn to bitterness if left untreated. Please know that I am not lacking compassion or empathy for life's challenges. Jamie and I have experienced our share of them. At some point, honest evaluation and assessment is necessary. If you happen to be stuck, my prayer is that the Holy Spirit will not only provide you a special "moment" that offers renewed faith and hope in your situation but will also lead you out of being stuck in your spiritual journey. God is not only able, but He is also willing!

My goal remains the same: to encourage you in your generosity journey.

Several years ago, I traveled to Greece and was able to experience Acts 18:1 for myself. After a day of touring Athens, including Mars Hill (where the apostle Paul had delivered a powerful presentation of the gospel), we traveled to Corinth, as the apostle Paul had. It became obvious to me that the seaport town of Corinth would have been a thriving and prosperous place. As I toured the ancient remains, Paul's two letters to the church at Corinth began to come alive to me, in particular this passage in 2 Corinthians 8:1–5:

> Now I want you to know, dear brothers and sisters, what God in his kindness has done through the churches in Macedonia. They are being tested by many troubles, and they are very poor. But they are also filled with abundant joy, which has overflowed in rich generosity.
>
> For I can testify that they gave not only what they

could afford, but far more. And they did it of their own free will. They begged us again and again for the privilege of sharing in the gift for the believers in Jerusalem. They even did more than we had hoped, for their first action was to give themselves to the Lord and to us, just as God wanted them to do.

In this passage, Paul is leveraging the impoverished and distressed church at Macedonia to challenge the believers in Corinth "**to excel** also in this gracious act of giving" (2 Cor. 8:7). This word "excel" used by Paul means to be exceptionally good at or proficient in any activity. Another way to describe the apostle's challenge to the Corinthian believers is that he desired for them to become exceptionally good at generous giving. Their acts of generosity were obviously lagging behind and not in pace with their spiritual maturation in many other areas. It is my thought that Paul adopts a no-excuse approach to address the lack of generosity within the church at Corinth.

Stuck people make excuses.

The beauty of the Macedonian believers was that they offered no excuses to not be generous. Notice both their challenges and their (re)actions despite their challenges:

> They were being tested by many trials.
> They were very poor.
> They were filled with abundant joy.

They overflowed in rich generosity.

They gave more than they could afford.

They gave out of their own free will.

They gave themselves first to the Lord and to each other.

Using the Macedonian model, Paul was urging the Corinthian believers "to excel" in their own generosity. He commended them for their many wonderful attributes but pressed them on the issue of generosity. This is the essence of my passion for this book. It is a call to all believers, especially in America. Let it be said of us that we did not make excuses; rather, we were determined to *excel* in generosity. No excuses!

I would like to share some examples of modern-day generosity that we all can emulate.

Sydney Sows with Soap Sales

Sydney was a part of a key family in the church we pastored in Dunwoody, Georgia, for ten years and was only a child when we met her. Her first gift to missions came as a result of a missionary from Cambodia coming to our church. Sydney was in elementary school and had been saving for an American Girl doll, which cost about $100 at the time. She had $40 to $45 in her savings account. The missionaries were speaking about human trafficking and how they were rescuing children. The missionary stated that $40 would rescue one child. Sydney did not hesitate, as her little heart was touched. She wanted to give all her doll money, which she had in coins and dollars, to rescue one child from trafficking. She has been passionate about missions and rescue ministries ever since.

Sydney is now a college grad student; "a poor college student," she calls herself. In the best sense of the word, she is a proud young adult who accepts the responsibility of making her own way. In September 2020, Sydney again had her heart touched for missions—she had a God moment. Even though she struggled to make ends meet on a monthly basis, she made a $50 faith promise to missions. Her idea to raise the money was to buy a soap-making kit and make soap to sell. She was determined to give every cent above expenses toward her mission's goal. Her first attempt at soap making was a disaster. However, she didn't give up. She purchased another kit and persevered.

In the first month, Sydney made a $50 profit in soap sales and fulfilled her missions pledge. But she didn't stop there; she continued her soap business for missions. The name of her business is *Simple Suds by Syd*. When I interviewed her, I learned that over the span of a year, she had given $1,723 from selling soap! On occasion, her roommates would chide her to use some of her soap sales toward living expenses. Nope, she wouldn't hear of it.

In my opinion, Sydney is a modern-day example of the Macedonian believers. As Paul said of the Macedonians, "For I can testify that they [Sydney] gave not only what they could afford, but far more" (2 Cor. 8:3). As you might imagine, I am very proud to know this young lady.

The Sacrificial Giving Challenge

Another great example is my friend Lorenzo. Pastor Zo, as I like to call him, pastors a small, but significant congregation in Pojoaque, New Mexico. I first met him years ago at a large church conference, and we had an immediate connection, as we exchanged our mutual love and passion for missions. He mentioned that his was a small church with a big heart for missions, and he asked if I would come to help them with an offering for a special mission's project. Several months later, I traveled to Pojoaque to speak. That Sunday morning, there were twenty-one people in attendance. I sensed in my heart that this tiny church in the middle of New Mexico shared similar qualities with the church in Macedonia. The reality is that many churches with smallish numbers and resources think they cannot afford to give to missions. In other words, it becomes an excuse not to be a generous people. But this was not the case with Pastor Zo.

Let it be said of us that we did not make excuses; rather, we were determined to excel in generosity.

I had already shared with him the idea of having him and his church do a sacrificial giving challenge. The idea was to give up something or several things in the household budget for thirty days. Examples could be Starbucks, entertainment, restaurants, golf, manicures, or any kind of expendable income. In essence, it is a fast of sorts for missions. In lieu of spending on those items, the people would give that money toward the mission's project. While pastoring, I used this method countless times, with incredible results for missions. Pastor Zo liked the idea.

I asked him what his expectation was for the thirty-day campaign. I asked, "What is your reasonable goal? Your record goal? Your miracle goal?" His response was, "I think $500 to $750 would be a reasonable goal; $1,500 would definitely be a record goal, and a miracle goal . . ." He trailed off; I could tell he had not allowed himself to go there before. But he pondered for a few moments and finally said, "Wow, $2,500 would be a crazy miracle goal for our little church."

Crazy, maybe, but I was on board! We prayed together as we offered this challenge up before the Lord.

It was a special moment when Pastor Zo called me to share the results of the thirty-day campaign. He was so excited that his small, but significant congregation had raised over $3,000 toward their mission's project! Truly, a miracle of generosity had taken place in Pojoaque, akin to the Macedonian model. "For I can testify that they [Pastor Zo] gave not only what they could afford, but far more" (2 Cor. 8:3).

We Can Do Better

On occasion, I receive invitations to speak at churches going through pastoral transitions. I consider it a special privilege to do so, as I am able to tap my thirty-plus years of pastoral experience and minister to a congregation during a vulnerable season. On one such occasion, I was able to connect with a whole congregation of modern-day generosity examples. When a pastor of a church in Dallas, Georgia, retired, I was invited to speak a few times over a several-month timeframe. The church quickly found out that my lane was (and still is!) generosity, especially for missions. So they asked me to help them raise an offering for missions. The previous year, the church had given $6,000 toward a specific missions project. I suggested to the leadership that we do a sacrificial giving campaign and raise the same amount in thirty days. They loved the idea!

I spoke at the bookend Sundays for the thirty-day campaign, so I was able to see it all the way through.

When the day for the big announcement arrived, I could sense it was going to be a special day. The leaders were almost giddy with excitement. They had decided that I would find out how much was raised when it was announced to the congregation during the service instead of beforehand. They invited me to the platform as they announced that over $18,000 had been given collectively and sacrificially. Let me remind you, this was in the middle of a transitional period, void of a lead pastor. The confidence and momentum the congregation received that day was without measure.

A few months later, the church voted in their new pastor. In fact, my wife and I were present for the installation service. The new pastor expressed his excitement about leading a congregation that exhibited such a spirit of generosity. "For I can testify that they [the Dallas Church] gave not only what they could afford, but far more" (2 Cor. 8:3).

As I said, I have the privilege of speaking at many different churches, from very small to very large to everything in between. Regardless of the size and scope of an audience, the message does not change. I like to use the Macedonian model found in Sydney, Lorenzo, and the church in Georgia to issue this challenge to churches all over America: We can do better! And we can do more. We can absolutely be more generous, especially toward missions. In fact, we can do *more* better! Yes, I know that is improper grammar, but you get the idea. I truly believe that this can become a starting point for the Holy Spirit to work in the hearts of believers at a deeper level. No excuses!

Chapter 3 Takeaway

Jamie and I have overcome many of the excuses for why we shouldn't be more generous. We would like you to be inspired by our experiences. Take a few moments and pray that God would help you remove any excuses for why you can't be more generous.

CHAPTER 4   THE SEED

*"The most important day of the harvest is the day
you choose your seed."*
Sam Johnson

*"Any fool can count the seeds in an apple, but only God
can count the apples in a seed."*
Robert Schuller

A friend and mentor in my life, Sam Johnson, has raised countless millions of dollars over the past fifty-plus years to build Bible schools all over the world. Now in his eighties, he is relentless in the pursuit of his calling. One day as he was driving across the plains of North Dakota, he saw an advertisement for a seed company. I believe it read, "The most important day of the harvest is the day you choose your seed."

I believe this statement speaks to the importance of putting good seed into the ground for the express purpose of reaping a harvest. It paints a scriptural and spiritual portrait in our minds as a part of God's divine design for His creation. Just as there are no shortcuts to the unseen germination process from seed to sprout, similarly there are no shortcuts to God's processes in our lives.

I tend to gravitate toward simple concepts, which many times have profound implications. For example, Robert Schuller states, "Any fool can count the seeds in an apple, but only God can count the apples in a seed." At first glance, this may not seem like much. However, from a spiritual standpoint, I believe there is something quite profound here in this simple illustration. Here are the basic metrics for a typical apple:

> A typical apple core usually contains **5–8** seeds.
>
> The process from a seed to fruit-bearing tree takes between **6–10 years.**
>
> From a single seed, a tree can produce an average of **800–1,000** apples per season. The typical fruit-bearing lifespan of a tree is approximately **20** years. A typical apple tree has the potential of producing approximately **16,000–20,000** apples over its life span. One apple, containing **5–8** seeds, has the capacity to produce a harvest of between **80,000** and **160,000** apples.
>
> Therefore, **"Only God can count all the apples in one seed."**

It may seem trite or cliché to say that only God knows the potential of the harvest of our lives. But the truth of the matter is, only He really does know. It is the reason we live by faith and not by sight!

Making Room for God's Blessings

When Jamie and I moved to Charlotte in 1983, a small house became available for us to rent from a widow in the church. It was a good thing, as she made the rent affordable for our meager salary. The house was 950 square feet, with two bedrooms and one bathroom, perfect for a family of three. However, we would find out a few short months later that Jamie was pregnant with our second daughter, Kristy. Even still, we were able to make room for our wonderful new addition.

About a year later, the church was able to increase our salary, and we were able to buy that little house for $37,000. That was a huge amount to us back then, but we were grateful for the opportunity. Then in early 1986, we received the fantastic news that our third daughter, Keri, was on the way. Honestly, this news came as quite a shock to us. In our minds, we were out of space and desperately in need of a bigger home. So we began to pray and scour the market for a larger one we could afford.

There are no shortcuts to God's processes in our lives.

We thought we had found the perfect place, but our own home was not getting much attention from buyers. The truth was, we lived in a rough area of town. Two people had been killed in the neighborhood over the last few years. One August afternoon as I was mowing the lawn, I had a God moment. While mowing, I was meditating on our house situation when I heard these words in my "knower": "It's not the right time." It was followed by, "When it is the right time, you will not have to put your house on the market." I turned the mower off, walked into the house, and sat down at the table. As Jamie sat down, I shared with her what I felt the Holy Spirit had just spoken to me. After a few tears, she confirmed that it was the Lord. I called our Realtor, and we took our house off the market.

One October morning, about a month before Keri's birth, I was in the church sanctuary having my devotions when I had another God moment. I sensed the Lord say, "Make a list of what you want in a house." I must admit, I was taken aback by this request. This unique word I received had never happened before and hasn't happened since. But prior to taking our house off the market, Jamie and I had looked and discussed extensively what we wanted and needed in a home. It was not unusual for me to keep a legal pad handy during my devotions. I pulled it out and began jotting down our desired specs, and in a matter of moments, the list had grown to seventeen items. It even included a specific interest rate, which, as you might know, rates change daily.

I hurried home to my pregnant wife to share with her both the word of the Lord and my newly-formed prayer list. She didn't alter anything on it. Our mutual house requests were seamless. Almost every day for the next several months, I prayed over that list. Then one morning as I pulled out the list to pray over it, I had a strong sense that I should put it away and just wait upon the Lord's timing for it to be fulfilled. I can now look back and see that the seed of promise God had planted in my heart many months before was now germinating. I put the house prayer list in one of my desk files in my office, and it would remain there for another year and a half. On three separate occasions during this time, someone offered us a word of encouragement from Scripture. All three verses happen to be from Psalm 84. We wrote them down and kept them on our refrigerator:

> Even the sparrow finds a home, and the swallow builds her nest and raises her young at a place near your altar.
>
> Psalm 84:3

> When they walk through the Valley of Weeping, it will become a place of refreshing springs. The autumn rains will clothe it with blessings.
>
> Psalm 84:6

> For the LORD God is our sun and our shield. He gives us grace and glory. The LORD will withhold no good thing from those who do what is right.
>
> Psalm 84:11

In May 1988, almost two years after taking our home off the market, the Realtor with whom we had previously listed our home contacted us. He said, "I know this may seem strange and out of nowhere, but I have someone interested in your house. In fact, they would like to see it today." In a matter of hours, there was a showing and a full cash offer. In addition, the buyer would allow us to stay in our home for the current payment until we could find another one. All I could hear in my mind was the word of the Lord: "When it is the right time, you won't even have to put your house on the market." The seed of promise was coming to fulfillment, and it was time for a harvest!

Rest assured, God is at work in our lives even when we cannot see it.

Coinciding with the house scenario, the lead pastor I had served for almost five years announced his retirement. He shocked me when he said, "Brian, I believe you are supposed to be the next pastor." On July 10, 1988, that congregation voted me in as their lead pastor. I was a ripe twenty-nine years of age. My first official day as lead pastor was on Monday, August 1.

That same day, we closed on our new home. In all the excitement of the previous three months, the filed-away house prayer list never came to my remembrance. I had not seen it in over a year and a half. In fact, I had forgotten where I even filed it! But on this first day of August, while moving offices from my staff office to the lead pastor's office, I stumbled across the prayer list. Jamie and I sat in awed silence as we read over the list. Our new home exceeded every single item on the list—every item, except for one. You guessed it! The interest rate we received was the exact rate placed on the list almost two years before. An overwhelming rush of emotions hit both of us as we expressed thanksgiving to the Lord for His incredible faithfulness to His word concerning us. You see, the most important day of the harvest is the day you choose your seed, and only God can count all the apples in a seed!

In the coming days, we would literally move into the fulfillment of God's make-a-list promise to Jamie and me.

Promises and the Glory of His Timing

It has been my experience as a pastor as well as on a personal level that there is a struggle common to us all. It's being able to fully embrace the reality that God's timing is usually different than anticipated. On occasion, God will surprise us with an immediate result. This is a rarity, but it is special nevertheless. The true test of faith is when it appears that His timing is painfully slow. What I have come to know and value is that God's timing is always perfect in order to accomplish His ultimate plan and purpose. Further, His plan and purpose for us involves the lives of other people that we may never know or even meet. The Realtor we used lived in our neighborhood but was not a Christ follower. When I told him the reason we were taking the house off the market, he looked at me in stunned silence. But two years later, he was the first one to remind me of what God had spoken to me. In the final analysis, the whole experience ended up being an authentic spiritual witness to him.

God is working in our lives to first bring glory to Himself and then to make us a witness to non-believers. Rest assured, God is at work in our lives even when we cannot see it. The seed of promise is merely germinating until it is His perfect time for a harvest. The key is to put the seed of your time, talent, and treasure into good soil. As you do this, it simply becomes a matter of God's timing until you to reap a harvest! It is all about His timing.

I was fortunate to experience a deep appreciation and value for God's timing while in Bible school. One of my favorite courses in college was on the book of Acts. This course would serve to become one of the core pillars of theology in my life and ministry. By my junior year, I was into the substantive material in my Bible major, and I was like a sponge. My professor, Mrs. Breusch, and her husband, who also taught at Southeastern, had been long-term missionaries. They offered rich life experiences as well as a no-nonsense approach to theology. We, the students, were the benefactors of such a unique blend of experience and practical theology. On one such occasion, Professor Breusch shared a special insight regarding God's perfect timing from Acts 3 and 4.

The Man, the Miracle, and the Message

The following are my abbreviated class notes from February 5, 1981. They are what I wrote as I planned my first three-point message.

Chapters 3 and 4 are about a man, a miracle, and a message.

The Man:

Lame from birth

Forty years old

A beggar: He was placed daily at the gate Beautiful, which was the primary entrance into the temple.

Jesus would have passed by him on numerous occasions but never offered him healing. Why? Jesus did not heal him because it wasn't the right time! It would bring greater glory to God for Peter and John to heal him in Jesus' name, as opposed to it being another of Jesus' many miracles.

The Miracle:

The miracle performed by Peter and John was a sign that vindicated Jesus.

It testified that Jesus was who He said He was: the Son of God.

Jesus was proven correct through this miracle. The miracle was accomplished "in the name of Jesus," which authenticated Jesus' authority coinciding with Him being the object of this man's faith. "Through faith in the name of Jesus, this man was healed" (Acts 3:16).

It also proved that even though Jesus was gone, His same power and authority is in operation through His disciples.

The Message:

The miracle provided the opportunity for the

message. "Peter saw his opportunity and addressed the crowd" (Acts 3:12).

The message: This Jesus you rejected is alive and well, and this man has been healed in His name! A call to repentance.

While speaking, Peter and John were arrested. The key purpose to God's timing: "But many of the people who heard their message believed it, so the number of men who believed now totaled about 5,000" (Acts 4:4).

The story of the healing of the lame beggar provides a very important insight into the ultimate plans and purposes of God as it relates to His timing. There were so many other times Jesus or the apostles could have laid hands on this man to receive healing. But the man had to wait forty years for his miracle. Needless to say, while sitting at the main temple gate begging and being an eyewitness to so many other miraculous events, he may have become spiritually calloused or desensitized. He may have even written off the possibility of ever receiving anything more than daily provisions through begging. Notice that on the day of his miracle, he was doing what he had always done: asking for money. There was no mention of asking for a miracle until it was offered by Peter.

The point is that after forty years of seeming barrenness, it was now God's perfect timing for this man to receive a miracle, which would bring ultimate glory to God and be a witness to countless unbelievers. So it is in our lives as well!

Only God knows the "when" of your harvest because He is in control of your harvest!

Wisdom in the "Waiting"

As mentioned, I am so grateful that this spiritual principle of God's timing was instilled in my heart as a young man preparing for full-time ministry. Friend, it has served me well and helped me through some of my own seemingly barren seasons of life. Proper spiritual perspective is a wonderful thing. Understand that the Holy Spirit oversees the timetable of your life in every way. Only God knows the "when" of your harvest because He is in control of your harvest!

One of the most difficult dynamics of pastoring for me was seeing people get sidetracked in their spiritual journey because God's timing did not align with theirs. Consequently, they would become either disillusioned, discouraged, disheartened or all of the above. In Galatians 6:9, Paul issues a caution against this very thing. He states, "So let's not get tired of doing what is good. At just the **right time** we will reap a harvest of blessing if we do **not** give up." Even as I write, there is a litany of names that come to mind of people I know from my pastoral years who fall into the "gave up" category. It really is a heart-wrenching thing.

The reality is that on this side of heaven, we have a limited scope of the big picture of our lives. I have always believed that each day is merely a snapshot or puzzle piece of the entire panorama of our lives. We cannot see or appreciate the whole picture by analyzing a handful of puzzle pieces. Only God sees the finished product. Faith is easy when we can see the results, but not so easy when our anticipated harvest is seemingly delayed. Always remember: "Only God can count all the apples in a seed."

Anxiety is neither associated with, nor a byproduct of, waiting on the Lord.

Several years ago, I did a study on the word *wait*. The most interesting nugget of truth I discovered came from a deep dive into the Hebrew word *qavah*. An important note when studying Hebrew is that it is a word-picture language. Each of the twenty-two letters in the Hebrew alphabet are associated with a word-picture. For example, the second letter in the alphabet is *beth*. The word picture for *beth* is a house or dwelling. Whenever it is used as a prefix, it simply means "house of." *Beth-el* means "house of God"; *Beth-lehem* means "house of bread." (Jesus was born in Bethlehem and claimed to be "the bread of life" [John 6:35, 48].) Every Hebrew word has a descriptive meaning associated with it.

The word *wait* has a descriptive word-picture meaning as well. It depicts one of several strands of rope being intertwined. It is the same idea found in Ecclesiastes 4:12, which says, "A threefold cord is not quickly broken" (MEV). I have always believed that you use Scripture to properly interpret Scripture. Isaiah 40:31

says, "But those who **wait** upon the Lord shall renew their strength; they shall mount up with wings as eagles, they shall run and not be weary, and they shall walk and not faint." When this verse is applied to Ecclesiastes, the strong implication is that those who are in "wait" mode, awaiting something from the Lord, are actually being spiritually strengthened in the process. This Hebraic idea flies in the face of the predominant western culture's concept of waiting, which usually has a negative connotation.

Further, I truly believe that when you are in a waiting posture for the Lord's timing in your life, this can truly be a victorious season of life. It can and should be a season of strengthening spiritually, mentally, emotionally, and even physically. Anxiety is neither associated with, nor a by-product of, waiting on the Lord. Rather, it is supposed to be just the opposite. It is in the waiting seasons of life that you can truly experience a peace that goes beyond comprehension, and a faith that is unwavering. Please be encouraged, my friend, as you wait for the promises of God to be fulfilled in your life.

Chapter 4 Takeaway

My heart for you is that you would reap God's blessings, especially when they seem to be delayed. Take some time to pray that God would help you to stand on His promises and wait on Him. May rest and strength rise up in you.

CHAPTER 5   THE FIRE

*"We can make our plans, but the L*ORD* determines our steps."*
Proverbs 16:9

I awoke to the screams from my oldest daughter, Lindy, that our house was on fire. It was approximately 5:30 a.m. on Wednesday, March 15, 2006. Little could I have known all the implications of that day. You see, the fire and its aftermath would become a hinge point for my wife and me. The fire actually set into motion a harvest season for us that we could never have imagined. We had been faithfully sowing seed for the last eighteen years, but it was now God's timing to bring about a harvest in a most unexpected way.

All three of our daughters happened to be home at the time of the fire. We had been planning to leave that morning for a spring-break trip to Lake Oconee, Georgia, which was about a four-hour drive from our house. Jamie was already up and about, preparing for a busy day of travel. Lindy was asleep in the finished basement when she awoke to flames shooting up the wall. (It would be discovered later that the fire was caused by a space heater plugged into a damaged extension cord.) Lindy immediately jumped up and alerted us all. As I sprang out of bed and rushed downstairs, I grabbed the fire extinguisher. In the meantime, Jamie and the girls grabbed what they could and exited the house. Our middle daughter, Kristy, who was planning her wedding in the next few months grabbed her wedding dress and the dog and ran across the street to the neighbor's house to call 911.

When I got downstairs and saw the smoke and flames, I attempted to engage the fire extinguisher but to no avail. I had pulled the pin, but in my haste, I was applying pressure to the wrong part of the apparatus. In hindsight, this proved to be a blessing, as the entire house was engulfed in thick black smoke in a matter of two to three minutes. I had just enough time to run back upstairs and grab my wallet, keys, phone, and a jacket. I was barefoot with no shirt on. I broke the door on the side of the garage to get our SUV and motorcycle out and pulled them into the neighbor's driveway. Then we waited for the fire department to arrive.

The girls were huddled in the SUV as Jamie and I stood outside the vehicle watching thick black smoke billow from our house. In that moment, a peace and serenity swept over me. As I was holding Jamie and looking at the girls, I muttered, "Everything that is important to me in life is right here, and they are all safe and sound." I had always believed that you can replace stuff, but you cannot replace precious life. I found it comforting to know that this was indeed the case. In a matter of minutes, everything we owned within our home was either destroyed by fire or damaged by the smoke. But there was a calm, as somehow we knew everything was going to be all right.

As part of their protocol, the fire chief interviewed me concerning the events of that morning. He asked what line of work I was in, and I told him I was a pastor of a local church. He then asked why I shut the door to the basement on my way out when I realized I could not get the fire extinguisher to engage. He confirmed what I had felt in that moment—that it was a good thing that the extinguisher didn't engage, as I would have lost precious time to get out of the house. I told him that closing the door just seemed to make common sense, and that it would slow the smoke from spreading through the rest of the house and offer a few additional minutes to get out safely. He explained that most people do not have the presence of mind to think about anything other than getting out of the house. He expressed that it showed leadership savvy to both react and process the situation in the moment. Beyond that, the simple act of shutting the basement door saved our house from burning down. Once the windows blew out in the basement, the draft from the upstairs would have pulled the flames straight up the steps, and the house would have been engulfed in flames in a matter of minutes. As it turned out, the basement was destroyed, but the rest of the house was spared any fire damage. We only had smoke damage. However, the thick black smoke damaged all the contents of the home, most of which had to be replaced.

The fire chief's voice took on a serious tone. He said, "Pastor, the daughter who was asleep in the basement is very fortunate." He went on to convey that in most cases, people are overcome by smoke inhalation before they can escape. An important caveat—

when I initially exited the house, I noticed Keri, our youngest daughter, lying face down in the front yard praying. We would later find out that she had a horrible dream during the night that our house was on fire and someone didn't make it out. She spent much of the night praying, as it had startled her so strongly. She was lying prostrate in the yard thanking God that even though we would lose all our stuff to smoke damage, everyone was safe. Thanks be to God!

The Lord was about to set the course for the rest of our life!

As mentioned before, the fire became a totally unexpected hinge-point event in our life. It connected the previous eighteen years with what would become the rest of our life and ministry. Although I will tell "the rest of the story" in the next chapter, for now I just want to share some of God's gracious provisions that are well worth mentioning.

Years before the fire, as I began to settle into my new role as the lead pastor in Charlotte, a wonderful thought occurred to Jamie and me. For the first time in our married life, we had some expendable income. It was quite liberating, to say the least. We came to the realization that we should open a savings account for unexpected expenses and three eventual college tuitions and weddings for our daughters (who were only six, four, and two at the time). A decision to open a savings account seemed to be the rational and responsible thing to do.

My life verse for decision making is Proverbs 16:9: "We can make our plans, but the LORD determines our steps." And the Lord was about to set the course for the rest of our life!

I do not remember the specific God moment, but somehow Jamie and I independently came to the same knowing that the Lord was challenging us to do something radical. Instead of placing our money into a savings account, we simply knew we were supposed to sow into missions. With that came a clear sense that when there were unexpected expenses, and when it was time for college and weddings, the Lord would provide for such. With no fanfare or announcement, we began to do what God had put in our hearts. Now, one might think this type of direction from the Lord would have been elaborate or bombastic, but it really wasn't. It was just a simple clarity of knowing that "this is the way [we] should go" (Is. 30:21). We would follow this specific giving path for the next eighteen years.

God's Miraculous Provision

I can look back now and wish I had better documented our journey during those eighteen years. But our life was so full with raising three kids, pastoring a growing church, and basically doing life, that we never gave it much thought. When we had unexpected expenses, the Lord provided for them every time, so we just took it in stride. Once we had set our course to rely on the Lord for the occasional surprises, like car and house repairs, braces, vacations, urgent care visits, etc., there always seemed to be a coinciding faith and trust that it was going be provided for.

Jamie and I came to the same knowing:
the Lord was challenging us to do something radical.

For the first ten years of our marriage, I do not have a recollection of taking a conventional vacation. Of course, we received vacation time, but we usually took that time to visit one of our families. This made sense to us because our only real expense was gas and a few meals along the way. And grandparents got see their grandkids. This was a win-win situation. One Sunday a few months after I had become the lead pastor, a wonderful couple approached me after service with a thoughtful and generous offer. They were part-owners of a beach house in Myrtle Beach, South Carolina. For their share in the beach house, they received twelve weeks a year, or one week a month every year. They stood there that morning with the schedule of their assigned beach weeks. Their offer to us was to pick one of weeks that best fit our schedule. For the next many years, until they sold their share in the beach house, the offer came to us to pick our week. We have many wonderful memories as well as home movies of those fantastic beach weeks. The beach house was a gift from God!

For years, my mom worked for a cleaning supply company. As part of her portfolio, she traveled extensively. As a result of her travels, she banked an ample supply of points with airlines, hotels, car rentals, and more. One year, she offered her points to us to take a family vacation. We had always wanted to visit California, so we made plans accordingly. We flew our family of five into San Diego, with the plan to work our way up the Pacific Coast Highway to reach our return flight out of San Francisco. The car we reserved was unavailable, so we were upgraded to a Lincoln Town Car. We stayed in nice hotels, drove a beautiful car, and went to Disneyland and the San Diego Zoo. The only things we paid for out of pocket were fuel, tickets to theme parks, and meals. I never figured out how much that trip would have cost us, but as you can imagine, it would have been costly and beyond our capacity. The California trip was a gift from God!

In September 1989, Hurricane Hugo ravaged the Carolinas. Even though the city was almost 200 miles inland, Charlotte was in the direct path of the storm. Regardless, the storm hit Charlotte with a vengeance, with 80–100-mile-per-hour winds. There was significant damage due to downed trees and power lines, and most of our neighborhood was without electricity for almost two weeks. We were fortunate, as we sustained no obvious serious damage to our home. However, a few months later, we noticed that the roof shingles were beginning to bow and bleed down the siding. We were not hopeful that insurance would cover the storm damages, because it appeared we were beyond the statute of limitation for hurricane damage. Nevertheless, I placed the call. It just so happened that our insurance company had an agent in the area servicing another similar situation. He came by and assessed the damage and decided that we were entitled to a full roof replacement and paint job for the exterior of our home. The insurance adjustment was a gift from God!

When Lindy turned eighteen, she desperately wanted her own car. We found a reasonably priced, late-model vehicle that she was thrilled with. We were able to scrape together the funds to buy it, but we had nothing for costly repairs should they come up. The car ran well for a year or so but started developing transmission issues. All the while, we were continuing our aggressive missions giving. We finally had to take her car in for repair. The estimate was almost $1,500 and would take about a week in the shop. There were a few times along our journey that we would have to put unexpected expenses on a credit card, but there was never a time we had to carry over a balance on it. We have always been able to pay off the balance when the bill came due. Further, we were never late on any monthly or regular bills. My plan was to put the cost of the transmission repair on a credit card and see how the Lord was going to provide. When the mechanic called us that Lindy's car was ready, we drove to the shop to pick it up. When I walked in, the gentleman behind the counter was smiling, and he handed me the keys and the bill that had "Paid in Full" stamped on it. I asked him, of course, who paid the bill, and the man responded, "He asked to remain anonymous." The transmission provision was a gift from God!

Our three girls were all born in November, two years apart from each other. We knew that when the college years rolled around, it was going to be extremely challenging to manage from a budget standpoint. In preparation, Jamie and I had made sure we had no car payments or any debt other than our mortgage. I drove a Jeep Cherokee with over 200,000 miles on it and a horrible paint job, and for a few years, Jamie drove a late model Buick Le Sabre. We committed to each of the girls to pay for three years of college. They would be responsible for the rest. When the cloud lifted after nine years, by the grace of God we had no college debt.

One of those years was extra challenging for us. I honestly do not remember the specifics, but we were coming to the end of the year, and we needed about $20,000 to pay off the school bills. This provision miracle was extra special because God not only provided what we needed for the college bills but went over and above, providing for some things we wanted to do around the house. We received a check for $32,000 out of the clear blue. The college funding was a gift from God!

Each God moment we have experienced on our journey has been unique. There really is no formula or timetable as it relates to God's timing for provision. The house fire and its aftermath reflect a culmination of an eighteen-year maturation process. But along the way, there were a few times that God did provide immediately.

When God asks for a seed, He always has a harvest in mind.

One example of an immediate provision happened in 1990. The year that I became the lead pastor in Charlotte, the missions giving was around $12,000 annually. I implemented a missions strategy using annual faith promises. That first year, I think our commitments were for $15,000. (We continued to set lofty goals, and we eventually surpassed $100,000 annually for missions.)

The second year, in 1990, I invited my former youth pastor and now missionary Terry Hoggard to be our keynote speaker. When Terry finished his message, I came to receive the faith promises. I sensed that I had a clear word from the Lord for someone. I said, "I believe God is speaking to a few here this morning to double your missions' faith promise from the previous year." As soon as I said those words, and to my complete surprise, I sensed that we were to be the first ones to do it. Before I could even process this moment, I heard myself saying out loud, "Jamie and I are going to be the first to double our faith promise." You should have seen Jamie's face on the front row. In my exuberance, I had just blurted it out. My saving grace was that she already had the same sense from the Lord to increase our giving.

Our first-year missions faith promise had been $75 a month. Our plan was that we would increase it as our income increased, which we did. However, doubling our faith promise to $150 monthly that second year was not in the budget. On the Monday morning after the missions' service, we were planning to lock in on a refinancing deal, as interest rates had been lowering. That same morning, one of my staff members told me that he had just refinanced his mortgage and suggested I speak to his lender. I made the call and found that his mortgage company was offering a better rate, so I decided to use them. The refinance took about thirty days to close. Upon closing, we realized that switching lenders resulted in an additional savings of $150 on our monthly mortgage payment. The resources to double our mission's faith promise was a gift from God!

God Always Has a Harvest in Mind

When you put the seed of your time, talent, and treasure into good soil, it will eventually produce a bountiful harvest. I have heard it said, "When God asks for a seed, He always has a harvest in mind." I believe this to be true. I also believe that there is no greater soil to sow into than the soil of missions. Jamie and I have followed this plan of sowing into missions for the entirety of our marriage and generosity journey. I have been asked on numerous occasions which part of missions is the most vital. Is it providing for orphans and widows, offering humanitarian aid, planting churches, building Bible schools, translating Bibles, digging wells, conducting evangelistic outreaches, ministering to the homeless, and so on? My answer is simply yes!

You are not responsible for all the world's needs, but you are responsible for some of them. The "some of them" is a matter of personal conviction in your own heart. I can promise that if you choose any kind of missions soil to sow into, you will not be disappointed. I have always believed that if people will be about

God's thing, He will be about theirs. God's thing is all about the lost and hurting in the world. Many times, you can find the lost and hurting in your own neighborhood. It is not a matter of either/or; it is both/and!

My hope for you is that as you continue reading, there will be some type of compelling God moment(s) that will inspire you on your generosity journey. Please take the opportunity to regularly evaluate the investments of your time, talent, and treasure. As you do, I am confident the Holy Spirit will be your guide.

Chapter 5 Takeaway

I want to encourage you that even in seeming setbacks, God is setting you up. Pray that He would help you recognize the principle of your time, talent, and treasure no matter what you may be facing. As you open yourself to new possibilities of generosity, you will see His provision!

CHAPTER 6   THE AFTERMATH

"We went through fire and flood, but you brought us to a place of great abundance."
Psalm 66:12

The hours, days, and weeks after the house fire were a blur of activity. One cannot be prepared for something one has never experienced. As pastors, Jamie and I had always been on the giving end of aid when there was a crisis in our church, and many times, we had led our church in aiding families who had lost everything in fires. Suddenly, we were now on the receiving end. In a matter of moments, we had no clothes (other than what we were wearing), no food, no shelter, and no toiletries, hair products, or makeup (for the ladies, of course). But there was an immediate outpouring of support from our neighbors and then, of course, from our church family. One of my lay leaders who lived close by brought me some clothing. As a keepsake of his generosity, I still have the pants and T-shirt I wore that day. There really was no time to experience an immediate sense of loss, as we were being inundated with an outpouring of love and support. To this day, it is still heartwarming to reminisce.

In addition to the love and support we received in the aftermath, there are several things that that were emblazoned onto our hearts. As I mentioned in the previous chapter, the fire became a hinge point in our lives because we were about to experience an unbelievable harvest!

On a practical note, we had a good homeowner's insurance policy that immediately kicked in. We were put into a hotel until temporary housing could be secured, and we were able to replace all the basic necessities. The girls were not disappointed to have to do an abundance of shopping over the next days and weeks. Jamie took the lead, working with the insurance adjuster, which was no easy task. Again, it is difficult to be prepared for something one has never experienced. Even though we moved back into to our newly remodeled home about four months later, it took about eighteen months before everything was completely settled. It was a daunting ordeal. On top of all the fire-related matters going on, we had Kristy's wedding to prepare for. Suffice it to say, our life was a whirlwind.

The Week After

The fire had happened on a Wednesday, but by Friday, we had already moved into an apartment, a place that would be our home for the next four months. The only personal possession I remember having at that time was my Bible. That first Saturday after the fire, as I sat on my Aaron's Rent-A-Center sofa, drinking my morning coffee, I opened my Bible to read devotionally. Wanting to get right into my reading, I literally began where my Bible fell open, in Psalm 66. I got as far as verse 12 when I was absolutely overcome with emotion: "We went through **fire** and

flood, but you brought us to a place of **great abundance**." I read this over and over.

I thought over the events of the last few days in light of the previous eighteen years for what seemed like an hour. The rush of emotion was like nothing I had ever experienced. About that time, Jamie came into the living room and could see I was a mess—in a good way. I could not speak. I gave her the Bible and merely pointed to the verse. In that very special moment, we did not need words to express the overwhelming awe and awareness of God's faithfulness. It seemed to us that before the Lord released His manifest harvest to us, He wanted us to experience His presence as it coincided with a confirming word.

Even now, more than fifteen years later, the majesty of that moment has not waned. In fact, whenever I share the fire story, I get to relive it every single time. I truly believe that this hinge-point moment became the launching pad for the rest of our life in ministry.

He wanted us to experience His presence coinciding with a confirming word.

A few years ago, I spoke at a church in Warner Robins, Georgia. A couple from the church in Hickory, North Carolina, had moved to Warner Robins and were in attendance that morning. We had known them during the time of the fire. During the message that morning, I shared our fire story. After the service, the couple came up to chat with us, at which time the husband pulled out a bulletin from our old church. It was from March 19, 2006, the Sunday after the fire! He had kept the notes from the sermon I gave where I had shared the story and the goodness of God. Our old friend seemed pleased that nothing had been embellished in the story. God really was and is that good!

Today, when I share the fire story in a message, I share an abridged version. But I have also put it in written form to be sure it is told in the same manner every time.

Another notable occurrence happened at the conclusion of the second service on that same Sunday morning, the weekend after the fire. There were several general contractors who were part of our church family, one of whom was Daniel McGalliard. After the service, he patiently waited while we were inundated with well-wishers and people offering their love and support.

Finally, Daniel's turn came to speak to us. I believe he was the last one in line. He said, "God told me to do the rebuild and the repairs on your house. Insurance will pay the general contractor 20%, but I am giving the 20% back to you." He would basically oversee the rebuild for no fee!

The floodgates of harvest had opened. We knew Daniel very well, as he and his family were faithful and active members of our church. This was not a reactionary moment of emotion by a church member. The way he spoke these words pierced our hearts. The Lord had chosen Daniel to be a tremendous source of blessing for us. Words cannot express our gratitude to the Lord and to Daniel for his obedience.

A third amazing thing happened, which came in three parts. We received three $1,000 checks from three separate ministries that we had supported through the years. I cannot say for sure, but I believe the checks arrived on three consecutive days. Even more exciting than that, the $3,000 was not needed for any immediate needs, as all our expenses were already met. When the dust—or the ash—settled, we would use the money to establish a savings account for the first time in our twenty-six-year marriage.

Even amid our dramatic harvest season, which was unfolding daily, we still faced many day-to-day challenges. A pet phrase I try to live by is, "Be prepared for the worst, but pray for the best." People who are not prepared for the unexpected twists and turns in life tend to get disillusioned and overwhelmed by setbacks that come their way.

Be prepared for the worst, but pray for the best.

Please do not misunderstand me. The apostle Paul references this preparation in Ephesians 6:13, which says, "Therefore, put on every piece of God's armor so you will be able to **resist** the enemy in time of evil. Then after the battle you will be standing firm." If you are prepared for these times and seasons of spiritual battle, you will see them for what they are by "standing firm" in the midst of them. Your expectation should be that God will always see you through, no matter how intense life's circumstances may be at times. Be encouraged, the Lord will always bring you through the battle victoriously!

Dealing with the Pests

Another way to explain the need to be ready "to resist the enemy" is with another seed-harvest metaphor. I like to call it "tending the trees." Invariably, there are all types of bugs or infestations that you may have to deal with from time to time. They are better known as pests. Most times, these are not fatal to the tree or crops. However, if left unattended, they could become a serious problem. When the unexpected critter comes around, it simply requires some attention. In other words, you must be prepared for the unexpected and not become overwhelmed by it. Unfortunately, it is often a necessary part of the process to reach your harvest.

For the past two years, our neighborhood has had an invasion of Japanese beetles. If left untreated, these beetles can destroy plants or trees by devouring the leaves and attacking the branches. In the first year, it took only one application of a liquid product on every plant and tree on our property to be rid of them. In the second year, however, they were much more aggressive. I had to spray everything at least three separate times during the summer months. In addition to the beetles, our homeowner's association notified us that our neighborhood was infested with army worms. I had never heard of such a thing before, but they can completely destroy a healthy lawn. We were fortunate not to experience the worm invasion, but some of our neighbors were less fortunate and had their lawns turn brown almost overnight!

For the annoying pest issues we did have, we had no warning or foresight. Regardless, these pests still demand our time and expense whether we liked it or not.

What is the spiritual application here? Simply stated, at times you will have to contend with spiritual pests even as you are reaping your harvest. The thief never stops trying to "steal and kill and destroy" (John 10:10). It is annoying to be spiritually sidetracked with the unexpected hassles that pests try to bring into our paths, and it requires time and energy that we would rather have so we can enjoy the harvest.

This is exactly how we felt. On one hand, unprecedented blessings were coming our way. But on the other hand, we were having to deal with the practical challenges of losing most of our possessions, living in short-term housing, having our daily routines turned upside down, and trying to prepare for a wedding. Jamie had to deal with the greatest amount of stress and challenges, by far. I marveled at how she handled all the distractions while keeping pace with being my wife—a pastor's wife—and a mother. As some might say, she was a rock star! In the end, all the pests were dealt with and ultimately were not able to detract from our harvest.

To be candid, there have been no lack of challenges, or "pests," during this entire book-writing process. In fact, I was quite naïve as to the detailed processes involved in completing this book. Once I had completed all the prep work and began writing, I really expected the wind to be in my sails with limited distractions. The truth was, however, I had overlooked what I have just shared—to be prepared for the worst. Somehow, I thought there would be a moratorium on distractions and pests. I woefully underestimated the potential for challenges. In hindsight, I should have put more emphasis on being spiritually and emotionally prepared for potential distractions along the book-writing journey. But God has promised that His grace is sufficient to see us through every situation! We have held fast to this promise!

So what are these "pests" we encountered recently? At the midway point of writing this book, Jamie had been to the emergency room on two separate occasions, as she is dealing with a serious health issue. At the time of this writing, we are still awaiting a firm diagnosis after a myriad of exams. I plan to provide an update in the epilogue.

For me, it is heart-wrenching to watch my bride of forty-plus years suffer. I have adjusted my travel schedule to stay close to home and care for her. As one can imagine, it has been extremely challenging at times to refocus on my writing assignment. We were experiencing a full array of pests that were designed to distract and disrupt.

Of course, during this ordeal, we have experienced a wonderful outpouring of love, concern and, most importantly, prayers for Jamie's healing from so many of our family and friends. We are indebted!

His provision for unexpected expenses along the way has always been supplied.

Many times, when I need to clear my head, I head over to the driving range and hit golf balls for a while. I find it therapeutic to pound those little white balls into submission as I put in my earbuds and listen to music. It gives me some good think time. On one such occasion, about seven months into the book journey, I had a God moment. The Lord impressed upon me that this book was going to be a great blessing to many people, and the enemy of our soul was trying to sidetrack us from our assignment. (Forgive me if this sounds haughty; I do not mean it to be, but I want to share exactly what I sense.) I sensed that Jamie and I were in the middle of intense spiritual warfare. In that moment, a peace came over me, and I knew that everything would work out for His glory. I also knew that we had to press on during our challenges. There came a knowing that the Lord was in control and that He would deal with the pests.

As I mentioned, the four months between the fire and the wedding were a blur of activity, adjustments, challenges, and distractions. However, in the midst of it all, there were countless blessings! Just one week before the wedding, we moved back into our "brand-new" home. It had been renovated and treated for smoke damage and was just amazing. The only thing that had not been addressed was the landscaping. It had been seriously neglected and abused during the four months of renovation. Early in the morning after we had moved in, I looked out the window and saw an entire landscape crew in our yard! Our good friend, Ken Warnes, had hired the workers and had provided all the landscape materials at his own expense. They worked all day and well into the evening, and when they were finished, our yard was a spectacular sight to behold!

One week later, our beautiful daughter was married, and the wedding and reception were amazing! A special keepsake moment that stands out for me some fifteen years later is a text message we received from our daughter Kristy just before she and her new husband, Taylor, boarded the flight for their honeymoon. She expressed her sincere love and gratitude for a "wedding/reception that was better than anything [they] could have ever dreamed." Because of the fire, the wedding had been completely paid for, and we had savings for the first time in our married life.

Over the next few years, we would begin to experience a new phenomenon in our lives. The more we accelerated our giving, the more the Lord buffered our savings. In other words, His provision for unexpected expenses along the way has always been supplied before we needed to turn to savings. This has been the case ever since that hinge-point moment when the Lord gave us the promise of Psalm 66:12: "We went through **fire** and **flood**, but you brought us to a place of **great abundance**." God is so faithful!

A Faith-Promise Blessing

A few months after the wedding, Jamie and I were sharing one vehicle. We now had two of our three daughters finished with college, and we felt a bit more breathing space in our budget. So we decided it was time to purchase a new vehicle for Jamie. She was so excited!

We were gearing up to begin the car search, when it came time for our annual missions faith-promise Sunday. The guest speaker that morning was my mentor and spiritual father, Pastor Hugh Rosenberg. The title of his message was "Faith-Promise Living," in which he talked about his own generosity journey. He believed and lived by the idea that the largest payment in our household budget should be missions. Jamie and I were mesmerized by his incredible examples of generosity for missions, and we were ruined for the ordinary that morning.

As we got ready to fill out our faith promise, Jamie leaned over and said, "We can go another year without a second car. I think we should take the money we set aside for a car payment and increase our faith promise by that same amount." So we increased our faith promise by the amount of the car payment and continued to share one car for the next year. Increasing our giving at this point meant our giving was now at an accelerated pace.

A year later, almost to the date of our decision to increase our missions giving, I received a call to go to lunch with one of the very generous givers in the church. He was a successful businessman and had an array of beautiful vehicles. In fact, he picked me up at the church in a brand-new Hummer. As we were enjoying lunch, he said, "God has woken me up three nights in a row telling me to give you a car."

I mentioned earlier that when God asks for a seed, He always has a harvest in mind. Since Jamie had foregone a car the previous year in order to accelerate our missions giving, the Lord was about to bless her for it!

We drove to Ron's house, and one of the garage doors opened. He referred to this vehicle as his baby. It was a beautiful 7-Series BMW! He handed me the keys and the title, and I drove home to show Jamie her new car. We never bought into a give-to-get theology. However, when you sow good and generous seed, God takes notice. There was no coincidence to this blessing. Ron was and is an excellent example of someone practicing the generosity gene. Because he acted on his God moment, we were able to experience our God moment. What a beautiful picture of generosity!

Chapter 6 Takeaway

My stories about the spiritual pests in life and how we choose to deal with them are meant to inspire and challenge you. Maybe you have some pests right now that are preventing you from seeing how you can possibly give of your time, talent, and treasure. Be encouraged that there is a way forward! Take a moment to pray that God will show you how to trust Him.

CHAPTER 7   THE KEYS

"Everyone can do some, some can do more, and a few can do much."
Brian Campbell

During my thirty-year tenure as a lead pastor, I recognized the importance and value of utilizing an occasional guest speaker so that the congregation could hear a fresh voice and perspective. If a speaker really resonated with our people, I would bring them back on occasion. One such speaker was Dr. Michael Brown from Branson, Missouri. He connected very well with the Hickory Church, and the Lord used him on several occasions to share something that had a keen prophetic edge.

In January 2003, during a Sunday morning message, Dr. Brown paused, looked directly at me, and made this statement: "Pastor, I don't know what it will be, but God is going to give you a key that will unlock new dimensions to this church and to your ministry." Without missing a beat, he flowed right back into his message. He and I never discussed the word he spoke to me, but I filed it in my heart and decided that when it was time for the Lord to share this key with me, it would simply happen.

Several months later, on my birthday, I awoke out of a deep sleep with a phrase going over and over in my mind: "Everyone

can do some, some can do more, and a few can do much."
I immediately knew this was the key that Dr. Brown had
referenced. This simple yet profound idea would ultimately
impact every area of ministry in our church. It would eventually
be adopted by several other churches as well. One area that was
dramatically impacted by the implementation of this principle
was giving. A fresh spirit of generosity was unleashed both in the
church as a whole and in our personal lives.

Turning the Key

We began to apply this concept of "everyone doing some"
to every key area of church ministry. Initially, the area most
affected was the prayer ministry. We had had a small prayer
gathering of ten to twelve faithfuls every Saturday evening for
several years. As I began to share the vision of one hundred
percent participation of "some," the people responded in kind.
We subdivided the church into four units/teams and asked each
member/attendee to participate one Saturday a month to serve as
the prayer covering over all things church related for that week.
That first Saturday, we had over one hundred people show up
for the prayer service. God's "man of power and faith," namely
me, could not believe his eyes. I was gloriously shocked by
what I saw! For the remainder of my time in Hickory, we would
average between seventy-five to one hundred people attending
prayer service every Saturday evening. It absolutely changed the
trajectory of ministry in that church.

> *Making our time, talent, and treasure available to the Lord almost always begins with "some."*

Historically, around 20 percent of people who attend church do 80 percent of the giving and serving. The Hickory church was no exception to these percentages. For the first few years I served as pastor, we were a 20/80 church. However, when we implemented "everyone doing some," the metrics changed significantly. With no exaggeration, between 75 to 80 percent of the church became involved in serving ministries, and our overall giving rose at the same rate. As with any church, there are casual attenders and outliers. They of course did not participate. Over the next few years, the church grew rapidly, and we expanded our campus to make room for the new growth. As it turned out, this single key truly set the tone for the rest of our entire pastoral ministry.

I strongly believe that making our time, talent, and treasure available to the Lord almost always begins with "some." If we are not willing to begin serving, praying, or giving "some" of what we have, the reality is we won't advance to "more" and surely not to "much." I also believe this key that the Lord imparted to me almost twenty years ago has proven to be a *master* key for my life and ministry. I am truly humbled and grateful to the Lord for entrusting me with such a special gift and calling.

As I look back and ponder the impact of this simple key, it begs the question: "What would have been the impact if I had not acted upon this revelation?" Would my personal life and ministry be different? How many people's lives would have been adversely affected? How much kingdom work would not have happened? Of course, we can only speculate because there is no way to know some things on this side of heaven. However, it is my opinion that the impact would have been startling. When God reveals these key moments in our lives, He typically has a much grander scheme in mind. He wants to affect not only our own personal lives but also the lives of so many others we may or may not ever know. In other words, a key can unlock doors of blessing to countless lives within the scope of our influence.

Unlocking the Miracles

When I was pastoring, I preached a message series titled "God Still Does Miracles." I built the series around a single key thought: *If we will do the difficult thing, God will do the supernatural thing.* The big idea is that there are select times in our lives that God chooses to unlock doors of blessing and/or opportunity through specific acts of faith and obedience. During the message series, I offered both personal examples and three stories from 2 Kings 3–5. Each story illustrates and reinforces the key—or a difficult thing required—to unlocking a door of blessing. It is my hope that these biblical stories will encourage you to study and research them in further depth.

They soon discovered that their obedience was the key to unlocking the door to their provision.

CHAPTER 7   THE KEYS

The first story, from 2 Kings 3, finds the kings and armies of Judah, Israel, and Edom heading to the land of Moab to go to war with the Moabites. About a week into their journey, they found themselves and their countless thousands of troops and livestock in the middle of the wilderness with no water. They were in an utterly desperate situation. They called upon Elisha the prophet who, in turn, called upon the Lord for divine intervention. (It is noteworthy that Elisha was involved in all three stories.) This particular word from the Lord was probably not what they were expecting:

> Thus says the LORD, "Make this valley full of trenches." For thus says the LORD, "You shall not see wind nor shall you see rain; yet that valley shall be filled with water, so that you shall drink, both you and your cattle and your beasts.
>
> 2 Kings 3:16–17 NASB95

You see, before the miracle provision of water was to be provided, there was something required of them, a difficult thing. I am reasonably certain that the last thing they wanted to hear from the Lord was to dig trenches in preparation for the provision of water. They must have been quite weary from the journey and parched from a lack of hydration. But in obedience to the word of the Lord, they began to dig! They soon discovered that their obedience was the key to unlocking the door to their provision.

The next morning, every trench was completely filled with water, just as Elisha had predicted. This was a bona fide miracle! There had been no wind or rain. Where did this water come from? Here is my theological speculation: Genesis 2:5–6 states, "For the LORD God had not yet sent rain to water the earth, and there were no people to cultivate the soil. Instead, springs came up from the ground and watered all the land." At the place of their greatest disparity and desperation, God had already gone before them and made preparation for their provision. He, in His omniscience, knows the what, the where, and the when of our needs from the foundation of the world. These kings and their armies were willing to do the difficult thing, which unlocked the door to their supernatural provision. It is my held belief that the degree to which they had prepared for the provision was in direct proportion to their expectation. In other words, their expectation determined the level of their preparation.

Expectation Determines the Level of Preparation

The second example, found in 2 Kings 4, tells of a widow who was also in a desperate situation. Her husband had worked for Elisha and had just passed away, leaving her with two sons. She appealed to Elisha for help. The prophet asked, "What do you have in your house?" (2 Kings 4:2 NIV). This poor widow said she had nothing more than a small jar of oil. Creditors were ready to seize her two sons as payment for her debts. She needed an immediate miracle of provision! However, Elisha required her to do something—a difficult thing.

The widow and her sons were instructed to go to all their neighbors and borrow as many empty containers as possible. Once they had collected them, the woman was to begin pouring the oil into them. That poor widow woman must have had some skeptical thoughts as she compared the small vial of oil to a room full of empty vessels. But then she must have thought, *What do I have to lose by a simple act of obedience?* As she began to pour the oil, something amazing and supernatural began to transpire. The oil continued to flow from that small jar until every single container was filled to the brim! When the last one was full, the oil ceased to flow.

It is clear to see that the widow's expectation determined the level of her preparation. The prophet then told her, "Go, sell the oil and pay your debt, and you and your sons can live on the rest" (2 Kings 4:7 NASB). God simply took what she had and multiplied it until her need was completely met. She was willing to do the difficult thing, which unlocked the door to her miraculous provision.

It is clear to see that the widow's expectation determined the level of her preparation.

The third illustration is from 2 Kings 5. The backstory is interesting, as a man in need, Naaman, had no obvious connection to the prophet Elisha. Naaman was a captain in the Syrian army and had leprosy. Apparently, a young Israelite girl had been taken captive by the Syrian army and had been assigned to serve in Naaman's household. One day, she mentioned to her master that there was a prophet of Israel who could be a liaison to his healing. As the story unfolds, Naaman and his entourage journeyed to Israel to find this prophet Elisha. The word of the Lord to Naaman via the prophet was, "Go and wash in the Jordan [River] seven times, and your flesh will be restored to you and you will be clean" (2 Kings 5:10 NASB).

This story prompts a different reaction than the previous two. It is pure supposition on my part, but my thought is that Naaman was not in a desperate situation, in need of an immediate miracle. He had the luxury to process the information and respond accordingly. His initial reaction to the prophet's instruction was one of anger and indignation. He set himself to depart and had no palpable intent of dipping seven times in the river. But his servants who had traveled with him offered some wise counsel. In essence, they said, "What do you have to lose?" We see once again that God chose a very specific key of obedience to unlock a door of supernatural blessing. Second Kings 5:14 says, "So he went down and dipped himself in the Jordan seven times, in accordance with the word of the man of God; and his flesh was restored like the flesh of a little child, and he was clean" (NASB). This story reflects just how difficult a thing it was for Naaman to respond in obedience to ultimately receive his miracle.

Doing the Difficult Thing

Recently my message series "God Still Does Miracles" became oh-so-real in my life. Our home church in Douglasville, Georgia, was celebrating its twenty-year anniversary, and Jamie and I were able to attend the weekend festivities. Pastor Dave shared with the congregation that a Kingdom Builders missions offering was about to be received. As soon as he mentioned it, these words flashed into my mind: "If you will do the difficult thing, I will do the supernatural thing." In that moment, I knew I was supposed to give $1,000. Before I could talk myself out of it, I did it! Jamie just smiled and shrugged her shoulders as if to say, "God's got this!"

The few months leading up to the offering had been tumultuous financially. We had been hit with several significant and unexpected expenses. One of those expenses was a $3,000 bill. Another was for a dental implant—also a large expense. Jamie and I needed a financial blessing, but we knew that the $1,000 missions offering was our "difficult thing," the key that we needed to unlock a financial blessing. That's exactly what happened!

God chose a very specific key of obedience to unlock a door of supernatural blessing.

Within thirty days of sowing that missions offering, two checks came unexpectedly. The first came just a few days before the $3,000 bill was due. And guess what—the check was for $3,000. Exactly what we needed! I received a note with that check that read:

> I pray the Lord blesses and continues to anoint your efforts with fruit that remains and finances for the kingdom effort as well. We value you and treasure the work you are doing for missions.

Jamie and I were floored at the specificity of the provision from the Lord! I mentioned earlier in the book that faith never gets any easier no matter how many times you have experienced the blessing of obedience. The flip side is that the exhilarating joy that coincides with God's faithfulness and blessing is unmatched every single time.

But, for us, it didn't stop there.

A week later, we were visiting some dear friends in North Carolina who were dealing with the tragic death of their twenty-two-year-old son. During our visit, they invited a young businessman and his family to join us for lunch. I sat and listened to this businessman's story of coming up through the ranks of the car business and the dream he had to start his own company. He now owns and operates a very successful business. As he explained the trek of his success, he made a very revealing statement: "Everything I have is from the Lord. It is all His!" I was so impressed with his sense of value and purpose.

After lunch, we said our goodbyes; this beautiful young family was heading out of town, and it was time for us to return home to Atlanta. We offered up prayer together, and they left. A few minutes later, my friend told me that the man who had just left asked us to stop by his dealership on our way out of town, as he had something for us. The manager was waiting for us when we pulled in. He smiled, handed me an envelope, and said, "God bless you."

As we opened the envelope, Jamie and I sat in stunned silence and absolute awe. It contained one of the largest financial gifts we have ever received. What a mighty God we serve!

It is my thought that the key(s) moments throughout our lives are just that: moments. I have heard it said, "The opportunity of a lifetime is in the lifetime of the opportunity." I believe that God uses these divine moments, specific keys for specific situations, to test our faith and obedience to His instructions while also providing a special opportunity to unlock supernatural blessings only He is capable of providing. It bears repeating that my passion for this book is to inspire you to fresh faith and action in your generosity journey. It could be that the Lord is or has been impressing upon you some type of faith action. If so, find His courage to be bold in your pursuit. Always remember, "Your expectation determines the level of your preparation." Be strong and courageous, my friend!

Chapter 7 Takeaway

As you have been reading our stories, can you recall divine moments from your own life when you knew God was asking something of you and then you saw His faithfulness on the other side? If so, how did the principle of the key, or "difficult thing," play a part? If not, take some time to pray that you would clearly discern the key, or difficult thing, that the Lord has prepared for your provision.

CHAPTER 8   THE STUFF

*"For the stuff they had was sufficient for all the work to make it,
and too much."*
Exodus 36:7 KJV

I think the best description I have heard regarding the word "stuff" is that it is a collection of things. At first glance, this may appear to be an oversimplification of the scope of the possessions in our lives. But in the final analysis, a strong argument can be made that our stuff truly is just a collection of things. It is worth repeating that the stuff of our lives consists of our time, talent, and treasure.

Let me offer some scriptural context to this perspective on "stuff." The book of Exodus contains forty chapters, and almost half of them are dedicated to the elaborate details of the design, materials, and construction of the original tabernacle. However, God's plan to finance this exquisite dwelling to house the glory of His presence was quite simple. Exodus 36:7 depicts the simplicity of the financing plan, or "stuff" model, God gave to Moses: "For the stuff they had was sufficient for all the work to make it, and too much" (KJV). The New Living Translation explains it as, "Their contributions were more than enough to complete the whole project." In other words, what God had already placed into the hands of His people—the stuff—was more than enough to finance His kingdom work.

As stated, God's plan was simple! The people brought daily offerings of their stuff to the building site, which in turn was used to erect and furnish the tabernacle. Those who were skilled by the Lord did all the work as they gave of their time and talent. Everyone else participated by bringing free-will offerings from their stuff daily. Could it be that this has been God's simple plan for financing the work of His kingdom all along? It would be easy to conclude that the greatest use of the stuff in our lives is for kingdom advancement.

During my pastoral years, I developed a three-tier teaching grid to better understand the basic spiritual dynamics of giving. The three tiers include reasonable giving, sacrificial giving, and revelation giving. The rest of this chapter will be devoted to unpacking these three tiers. The grid not only helped me to communicate the progressive and maturation process of giving, but it also helped my congregation embrace where they might be on their own generosity journey. In recent years, I have been communicating this three-tier concept wherever I am speaking.

Reasonable Giving

The first tier begins with reasonable giving. This is a great place to begin but not a great place to remain. Notice that the root word in *reasonable* is *reason*. *Reasonable* can be defined as having sound judgment or being fair or sensible. It would be difficult to argue against being reasonable, especially in the context of generosity. However, the point here is that the whole of reasonable giving is in the realm of the intellect. The apostle Paul made a revealing statement regarding generosity in 2 Corinthians 8:12, which says, "The heart regulates the hands" (MSG). I will develop this thought later in the book, but it is worth noting that spiritual generosity is not ultimately regulated by reason; it should be regulated by the heart.

Reasonable giving understands that there is a responsibility as a Christ follower to be an active participant in giving. It is important to note that being reasonable is a subjective and relative term. Therefore, reasonable giving is a cognitive exercise determined by the individual. The caution at this level of giving is that the Holy Spirit is typically given little or no opportunity to be involved in the decision making regarding generosity.

Please understand that it is not my desire to seem critical or condescending with my observations; however, I do think it is important to be authentic and transparent based upon my experiences. But I believe that far too many Christ followers choose to abide in the land of reason as it relates to giving. There may be the occasional venture into sacrificial or even revelation giving, but by and large, they are firmly entrenched in the land of reason. As a result, they rarely—if ever—experience the thrill and joy that coincides with advancing into the other two tiers of giving. Suffice it to say, there is a considerable percentage of Christ followers who have not progressed beyond reasonable giving.

If you happen to be living in the land of reason and have not ventured into sacrificial or revelation giving, I trust you will continue to read with an open heart and mind.

Sacrificial Giving

The second tier of giving is sacrificial. Sacrificial giving is the place where the spiritual components of giving really begin to take shape. In recent years, I have become quite enamored and intrigued by this sphere of giving. I truly believe that sacrificial giving holds a special key that unlocks doors to untold divine authority, anointing, and blessing. I do not think I can overstate the possibilities that exist when we are willing to sacrificially offer our time, talent, and treasure. Sacrificial generosity is a breeding ground for the supernatural blessings of God to be released in our lives. In essence, the stuff of our lives is being made available and accessible to the Lord at a new level.

As a pastor, it had long been a desire of mine to use the Moses "stuff" model for a building or renovation campaign. The opportunity presented itself while I was pastoring in Dunwoody, Georgia, in 2009. When I became the lead pastor in late 2007, it was obvious that a significant portion of the campus was in desperate need of renovation, including the worship center. The challenge was that the church already had a large debt, making it virtually impossible to borrow any additional funds for renovation. At that time, I had never heard of anyone attempting to do a stuff campaign. As a result, there was nothing to emulate. We simply decided to follow the basic Moses template.

I truly believe that sacrificial giving holds a special key that unlocks doors to untold divine authority, anointing, and blessing.

The campaign was both an overwhelming success and, coincidentally, a bit of a nightmare. The people responded with great generosity by bringing in their stuff. What we had not properly planned for was the temporary storage and liquidation of everything that was rapidly being donated. Some of the items given during that three-month campaign were—

a car
a motorcycle
a school bus
a jet ski and trailer
furniture
jewelry
land
stocks
savings
retirement funds
legal services

We were able to completely renovate the worship center as well as some additional rooms surrounding the main auditorium. It still warms my heart to remember the incredible outpouring of sacrificial generosity from our congregation during that campaign.

Jamie and I took inventory of our own stuff and decided anything that was expendable and of value we were going to give. It started with my beautiful Electra-Glide Harley Davidson motorcycle. It was tricked out with Samson pipes, LED lights, lots of chrome, and other bells and whistles. The Sunday morning we launched the campaign, I literally rode it down the center aisle and parked it in the front of the worship center. I have always believed that leaders lead, and they do so by example. At that time, there was no greater valued personal possession I owned than my Harley. Additionally, we gave a piano, furniture, a Browning hunting rifle, jewelry, and other miscellaneous items. A purge of stuff is a healthy practice on occasion, especially when the Lord asks for it! I can honestly say that we never had any regrets on what we sacrificially gave.

It was no coincidence that we were audited by the IRS that same year. The only part of our tax return they wanted to see proof of was our contribution statements. They requested proof of all of our charitable contributions. After some time, the IRS returned our records with an assessment of their findings. They did find one mistake. However, they found something we had failed to properly claim. As a result of the mistake . . . they sent *us* an additional check. It was the exact amount we had previously given to a struggling pastor couple.

CHAPTER 8   THE STUFF

I like to say, "God keeps the books!" I remember reading something Chip Ingram said in his book *The Genius of Generosity* that captured the essence of sacrificial giving best. He explained that God's "genius" in generosity is that He guards against greed by blessing us when we give away what we have.

Revelation Giving

The third tier of giving is revelation giving. In many respects, sacrificial giving is a bridge from the land of reason to the promised land of revelation. Here is what I mean by this statement. The land of reason and sacrifice are based largely in the natural realm. We decide what we will give, when we will give, where we will give, and for how long we will continue to give. In all candor, the generosity decisions we make are derived within ourselves. Revelation giving is unequivocally initiated and inspired by the Holy Spirit. These become the God moments along our generosity journey. Whereas reasonable and sacrificial giving originate in the mind of the giver, revelation giving is prompted in the heart of the giver by the Holy Spirit. Let me offer a few personal and corporate church examples of revelation giving.

I once heard it said that you will never lack in the specific areas of your generosity.

Jamie and I made the decision early on in our marriage that whenever possible, we would bless others with our stuff instead of selling it. We never gave away junk, only good usable items. We have given away multiple vehicles, furniture, furnishings, collectibles, gold coins, cash money, etc. We made the decision to make our stuff available to the Lord whenever He prompted us to release it.

I once heard it said that you will never lack in the specific areas of your generosity. I'm not quite sure as to the full validity of this statement, but I do have an uncanny example. Since my college days, I have enjoyed playing golf. In the early years of our marriage, I had an old, pieced-together set of clubs. After many years, I was able to buy a brand-new set of irons that were the latest and greatest on the market at that time. About a year later, I hired an associate pastor who was just beginning to golf. One day, we went to the driving range to hit a bucket of balls. In a moment, I sensed the Holy Spirit prompt me to give my fairly-new set of irons to him.

As we were getting ready to leave the range, I reached into my golf bag, pulled the irons out, and handed them to my associate. He was a bit bewildered and didn't know what to say. I didn't mince words; I simply said, "God told me to give you my irons. Here ya go!"

This moment became a revelation or God moment for me. It also tied into what I learned from Ingram, that God guards us against greed when we give away what we have. Over the past thirty years, I have had at least twelve to fifteen full sets of golf clubs pass through my hands. I have given away brand-new clubs on many occasions, as well as clubs that were slightly used. All told, I can count on one hand how many golf clubs I have purchased during this same timeframe. One thing is for sure, I have never lacked for golf equipment!

Jamie and I have practiced a special Christmas tradition for many years. During the month of December, we set aside an amount of money, usually $1,000, and designate it for extravagant tips leading up to Christmas. Many times, we have simply left the tip without witnessing the response. But if we sensed it was a God moment, we would discreetly observe. We pray and ask the Holy Spirit to lead us to a restaurant server in need of a blessing. Two such events really stand out.

One year, we were out doing some Christmas shopping and decided to grab lunch. There were countless restaurants from which to choose, so we paused in the mall parking lot to pray and ask the Holy Spirit to lead us to someone in need. When we looked up, I could see a California Pizza Kitchen. We immediately knew this was the place! During lunch, we chatted with the server and asked if she was prepared for Christmas. She shared that she had taken on this extra job through the holidays in order to buy Christmas presents for her kids. We were struck with how upbeat she was. We left a $250 tip. As we exited the restaurant, we looked back through the window to see the waitress crying and being hugged by fellow servers. God is so faithful!

On another occasion, it was the week before Christmas. It had been challenging that year to find the right people to bless. I studied Google Maps and looked for a place within a ten-mile radius. We live in a metro area where there are countless hundreds of restaurant options within twenty to thirty minutes. An Italian restaurant we had never been to seemed to stand out. It was not at a convenient location for us, especially with traffic, but we sensed that this was the place we should go. The restaurant was crowded, so we had to wait a while to be seated. I noticed one server, and just by her mannerisms and body language, we could tell she was not into her job. I thought to myself, *I sure hope we don't get seated in her section.* Of course, she was our server!

Jamie and I looked at each other, and I knew we were thinking the same thing, *Wow, we really missed it on this one.* It took some prodding on our part to learn some of this young lady's story, but she finally began to open up. She was on her own, trying to work her way through college. It was obvious that the holidays were extremely difficult for her. We were so glad that we did not allow her hardened demeanor to deter us, because it became abundantly clear that she was indeed our assignment. We had never done this prior, but we handed her a $250 tip and asked her to look at it. That moment is both priceless and etched into our memory. She cried! We cried! We hugged her and told her, "God loves you so much that He sent us to you tonight. He has a wonderful plan for your life." This became a special revelation or God moment that began as a sacrificial offering.

There are other occasions when revelation giving depends completely upon the Lord to provide in a supernatural way.

A final example of revelation giving actually involved Jamie and me pledging to give and someone else footing the "bill." In 2004, we were pastoring a growing congregation in Hickory, North Carolina, and had embarked on a $1.5 million renovation/ expansion campaign to help facilitate our growth. All three of our daughters were in college at the time, and I was driving a Jeep Cherokee with 220,000 miles and a bad paint job; we were also still giving all our savings to missions. During the campaign, Jamie and I came to a "revelation knowing" that we were supposed to "faith promise" $40,000 to the campaign to be paid over three years. At the time, we barely had $400 to our name, let alone $40,000.

On the night of the banquet, a man who was not a Christ follower had come with his wife. He had attended services on occasion but was a casual observer at best. As he intently listened to me tell the story of how we came to a "revelation knowing" to faith promise $40,000, he decided that he would pledge $45,000 to "beat what the preacher was doing." Within thirty days of making that faith promise, the Lord spoke to a local businessman to pay our $40,000 faith promise in full. And the guy who pledged $45,000? He paid his commitment in full within six months!

The Overlap of Sacrificial and Revelation Giving

In many cases, revelation giving overlaps with sacrificial giving. The Lord will ask for something from the stuff of our possessions in a revelation or God moment. But there are other occasions when revelation giving depends completely upon the Lord to provide in a supernatural way. Again, I have many corporate church examples I could share, but I will share the two that are most meaningful to me.

I immediately had a God moment that our church was supposed to commit to the full amount.

In the early 2,000s, I had traveled to Bulgaria multiple times to speak at leadership gatherings across the country. During my travels, I met some world-class leaders who had amazing testimonies of how they came to Christ during the communism era. One such leader was Peicho, a man whose testimony could have been right out of the book of Acts! Peicho had planted a church in his hometown of Tryavna, Bulgaria, which for years, met in rented facilities, as banks would not lend money to churches. In order to buy a building, the church had to have the full amount for purchase. The church had been saving for many years to eventually purchase their own facility. Finally, the building they had been renting became available for sale. The challenge was that they lacked $21,500, and the full amount was needed in a very short period of time because there were other buyers interested. The window of opportunity was narrow.

During this time, the economy in our area of North Carolina was struggling terribly in the aftermath of 9/11, and our church finances were tight. When Peicho asked if we could help, I immediately had a God moment that our church was supposed to commit to the full amount of $21,500. I called an emergency board meeting and shared what God had laid on my heart. Thank God for leaders who can walk in fiduciary responsibility as well as walk by faith when its God's time to do so! They all agreed we should take this on and that the Lord would provide! However, Peicho needed the guarantee for the full amount before we could arrange to take up the offering. In the few days that passed, Peicho had received $2,000, but we were still committing to the remaining $19,500, an amount that still would have seriously depleted our general fund. The Sunday morning following the emergency board meeting, we took up a special offering. By this point in the book, you won't be surprised to know the amount that came in was exactly $19,500. God is so faithful!

The second example of a revelation giving at a corporate level is the last and largest I had seen during my pastoral ministry. This story requires some backdrop for context. As I look back, I can see how the Lord was gracious to not threaten my credibility with the three congregations I served whenever it was time to press to a new level of corporate generosity. In most scenarios, it was a hybrid of sacrificial and revelation giving. But this final example is not like the previous ones. With this exception, I always had a latitude as the key leader to appeal to the board and congregation for their participation. This time, God put it completely on me, and He was the only one capable of making it happen!

In July 2014, I attended a *Fire Bible* event. During an evening banquet, a special project was presented. During the presentation, I had a revelation or God moment. What came to my mind was the largest number I had ever committed my church to for a single mission's project: $50,000. A cold chill ran up my spine, as I knew this was the Lord. I also knew that there was no possibility of bringing this back to the church for consideration, as our missions budget was already fully vested for the year. With tears streaming down my face, I filled out the faith promise that I would give by the end of the year. Besides the *Fire Bible* personnel, Jamie was the only person who knew what I had done.

In mid-August, things got even more interesting. Another ministry asked me if our church would host a small missions gathering. We gladly accepted and prepared for the event. On the morning of the event, I performed a funeral service for one of our dear elderly saints. She was one of three sisters, all in their eighties, who lived together in their retirement years. They had attended church faithfully and had a special heart for missions. Sadly, one of those sisters passed away, and I was conducting her funeral.

Later that evening, I hosted the missions event, and the next morning, we held a breakfast in which a special project was presented. It had been agreed that our only responsibility was to play host. I was not expected to give money also. However, as I sat there and listened to the presentation, my heart was gripped with an overwhelming need to respond. In that moment, I had a clear revelation that we, as a church, were supposed to faith promise $10,000. I had the exact emotional and physical feeling I had when I committed the $50,000.

When I handed the leader my response card, he looked at it and handed it back, saying, "No, no, no. You were gracious to host the event, and we agreed you would not faith promise for the project." I shoved the card back in his hand and said, "You don't understand. I do not have a choice because God told me to!" He reluctantly accepted the card.

The new faith venture would require our complete trust in Him, with no safety net.

Interestingly, it was not as difficult to make the second commitment of $10,000, but not simply because it was a smaller amount. I honestly thought, *God can provide $60K just as well as He can make provision for $50K.* I was not being flippant; I simply had a knowing that God was in all of this.

Over the next weeks and months, however, I had some real battles in my heart and mind as to whether I had really heard from the Lord. I began to feel irresponsible, that two different ministries were expecting these funds to come in, and I alone was responsible. I reached out to my staff and asked them to help shoulder the load in prayer.

We were fast approaching the end of the year, with no miracle of provision in sight. The church offices were closed between Christmas and New Year's Day, but I happened to drop by the office one morning. I believe it was December 28. My business administrator called me to see where I was at the moment. When I informed him I was at the office, he said he would be right over, as he had some news for me. He sounded excited, so I surmised it was an end-of-the-year financial gift to the church. Upon entering my office, he was grinning from ear to ear. He announced, "Pastor, your mission's miracle is about to happen."

I can still feel the rush of adrenaline I felt as he said those words, even before I knew what they meant.

He explained that the church would be receiving a check in the next few weeks as part of an inheritance. The inheritance was coming from the precious sister for whom I had performed the funeral in August, the same day I increased my missions commitment from $50,000 to $60,000. The two sisters inherited the deceased sister's estate, which included stock from the company where she had retired. They decided their deceased sister would have wanted something from her estate designated for missions. Because they did not know the exact value, but they knew it would be sizable, they waited until the estate was fully settled before they shared the news. The check amount would be $78,760.67! We would receive the money in mid-January, so I told both ministries they would have the funds I promised by the end of January. In addition, we were able to send a special offering to *all* the missionaries we were currently supporting.

Little did I know at the time that God was stretching our faith to prepare us for the next chapters of our life in ministry. The new faith venture would require our complete trust in Him— with no safety net. Candidly, I can see that up until 2014, I had always had a safety net as a pastor; I could go to my leaders and then to the congregation to participate and give to the vision the Lord was placing before us. This new step in our generosity journey would enter into new territory. We would have to trust the Lord on our own. The truth be told, I believe the Lord delights in this level of trust above all others!

Chapter 8 Takeaway

Have you ever had any revelation or God-moments that resulted in sacrificial giving of your time, talent, or treasure? If so, recount what took place. How were you impacted, and how was the recipient impacted? If you do not have a story like this, think about what you plan to do when you do have one. Perhaps pray that God will prepare you to step into sacrificial giving with confidence and trust in Him.

CHAPTER 9   THE GOAL

"If you aim at nothing, you will hit it every time."
Zig Ziglar

I believe the wisest beginning point for goal setting should be based in Scripture. The obvious reason for this is that it guards against self-serving goals that tend to reward one's own sense of accomplishment. There is nothing wrong with experiencing satisfaction for a job well done. Generosity goals, when founded in Scripture, produce a deep sense of kingdom accomplishment accompanied by a sense of fulfillment for doing it God's way! A perfect starting point for generosity goal setting is found in 2 Corinthians 9:7:

> You must **each decide** in your heart how much
> to give. And don't give reluctantly or in response
> to pressure. "For God loves a person who gives
> cheerfully."

The *Fire Bible* commentary notes expound on the word "cheerfully." It says that the Greek word (*hilaros*) "does not refer to loud and uncontrolled expressions of leaping and laughter. Rather, it means we get to experience an overwhelming sense of inner joy, gladness, and fulfillment that goes along with generous giving."

The process of giving begins when you decide in your own heart and mind what your generosity goals will be. Once you have set your course, it becomes an amazing journey, one filled with no regrets!

Generosity goals, when founded in Scripture, produce a sense of fulfillment for doing it God's way!

In my early thirties, I was part of an informal network of young lead pastors with young families. There was never any formal structure or agenda other than randomly connecting whenever we could. On occasion, our young families would get together for a day or two just to spend time together. As I reminisce about those early years, I can see how much iron sharpening iron took place in many of those casual settings. At one of these family gatherings, the men broke away one morning to play a round of golf.

While my friend Jim and I were riding together in the golf cart, the discussion turned to generosity and giving. He may have been the first person I confided in that Jamie and I were sowing all of our savings into missions. He was very encouraging and told me how he thought God would bless our life and ministry as a result. He then went on to make a statement that would forever change my approach to giving. Jim said, "My wife and I have set a 20 percent goal for our giving, and we eventually desire to give more to missions than the 10 percent tithe." I had never heard of anyone having actual giving goals before. I was absolutely captivated by the idea of setting one.

I cannot recall how many times since then that Jamie and I have discussed and carefully considered our generosity goals through the years, but suffice it to say, it has been a considerable amount. The first time, though, was the most memorable, as we thoughtfully and prayerfully considered the matter. After some period of contemplation, we finally set our initial giving goal at 15 percent. The goal was never on any type of timetable. Of course, our savings, which was already designated for missions, became our scale.

It took us about three to four years to reach that first giving goal of 15 percent. I remember experiencing such a feeling of joy and fulfillment for reaching that first goal. From there, we decided our next giving threshold would be 20 percent. Our plan to reach this new giving goal was to increase our giving by at least 1 percent every year. It took another four to five years to reach the full 20. Again, the overwhelming feeling of inner joy and satisfaction of reaching 20 percent was amazing. And to think it all started almost ten years before, during a random game of golf with my friend!

We realized that our generosity journey had become an essential and core value to who we were as Christ followers when we reached our 20 percent goal. It was a gradual awareness that a culture of generosity had been organically developing in our heart. Honestly, it just kind of happened! Innately, we just kept increasing our giving. As a result, we no longer felt the need to set specific numerical giving goals. Annually, we figure our total giving percentage when we submit our giving records to our accountant. Our giving has never receded but has continued to increase year by year. From 20 percent, our giving grew rapidly to 25 percent and progressed from there.

It was a gradual awareness that a culture of generosity had been organically developing in our heart.

I'm reminded of the story of a good friend of mine named Joe. He went to be with the Lord several years ago but left an incredible legacy of generosity. He had told me his story of a God moment he had experienced regarding generosity. He was a successful businessman who regularly gave 10 percent plus offerings for most of his adult Christian life. But one day, the Lord challenged him with this idea: Instead of giving 10 percent and living off the 90 percent, do the opposite. Joe was being challenged to live off of 10 percent and give 90 percent. So he did! With a glow of joy on his face, he said, "Brian, God has so blessed my life that I now live better off of the 10 percent than I ever did on the 90." Joe obviously had a radical generosity goal that was birthed in revelation giving. He truly believed the principle that you could not out-give God. Better yet, he lived it!

Developing a Culture of Generosity

I propose that developing a culture of generosity in your life, church, nonprofit organization, or business should be the primary goal. The irony here is that I have already admitted that our giving goals never included developing a culture of generosity. That culture merely became the outcome of reaching our shorter-term generosity goals. As a result, I have been developing a teaching series called "How to Develop a Culture of Generosity." These principles are applicable in our individual lives as well as in any business, church, or civic organization. The tentative outline for the series includes—

> Setting Your Course (Goal-Setting Safeguards)
> Develop a Strategic Plan (Three-Tiers-of-Giving Model)
> Strategic Plan Contingencies (Prepare for the Unexpected)
> Work the Plan (The Flywheel Concept)
> The Laws of the Harvest (The Untold Version)

It is my intent to offer this series as workshops. I hope that it, along with *The Generosity Gene* will encourage those pursuing their own generosity journey.

I propose that developing a culture of generosity in your life, church, nonprofit organization, or business should be the primary goal.

During my master's thesis research, I uncovered two valuable insights that draw a direct correlation between giving goals and spiritual development. In the book *Contagious Generosity*, Chris Willard and Jim Sheppard reveal two powerful spiritual dynamics of generosity. Here, I've condensed these thoughts:

> The real goal is spiritual formation. We believe that generous giving is one of the best external indicators for measuring transformation and spiritual growth. Nothing demonstrates the authentic spiritual growth of a believer more compellingly than spontaneous acts of generosity, welling up from a heart changed by the grace of God. Generosity, when motivated by a genuine love for God, is contagious, drawing others to wonder why people would give of themselves while expecting nothing in return. In fact, a life— and a church community—that is characterized by generosity may be the most compelling, effective evangelism strategy we have as followers of Christ. We believe that Christ followers who are pursuing generous lives provide the clearest picture of God to others.[12]

I wish to delve deeper into these two spiritual dynamics of generosity identified by Willard and Sheppard. The first is that a person's generosity is a measurement for his or her spiritual

---

12 Willard and Sheppard, *Contagious Generosity*, 41, 173, 175, 187.

growth. Second, living a generous life as a Christ follower is the clearest and most effective way to be a Christian witness.

The first dynamic strongly resonates with me—generosity is quite possibly the single best indicator for measuring spiritual growth. My thought process is that God's plan of salvation, as revealed in Scripture, shows the measurables of His generosity toward humankind:

> God so **loved** that He **gave** His very best in Jesus. (John 3:16)
> The penalty for sin is death. We are all sinners. (Rom. 3:23)
> God makes the payment for our sin through the **free gift** of Jesus. (Rom. 6:23)
> God **demonstrated** His love by sending Jesus while we were yet sinners. (Rom. 5:8)
> Salvation is provided exclusively by God's grace. It cannot be earned. (Eph. 2:8–9)
> Salvation is received by believing in our hearts and confessing with our mouths. (Rom. 10:9–10)
> When we confess our sins, He forgives us completely. (1 John 1:9)

If you have never asked Jesus into your heart, I urge you to not hesitate. Stop right now, turn to the "Prayer of Salvation" (page 185), and pray that simple but powerful prayer. Then come back here, and we'll continue.

Measurable Giving

Considering the idea that a person's generosity is a measure of spiritual growth begs a rhetorical question: If God's greatest act of generosity is measurable, how much more should our acts of generosity be measurable? The ingredients of generosity require faith, sacrifice, obedience, discipline, humility, and ultimately, a full trust in the Lord that He will perform His Word concerning us. There is only one place in Scripture, Malachi 3:10, where God issues a challenge to put Him to the test. It concerns the tithe, directly correlating a promise of God's blessing with honoring Him in your giving.

The second spiritual dynamic, that our giving becomes a platform to be a Christian witness to those who are not Christ followers, is extremely important. This places generosity at the crossroads of the gospel. I have a few close friends who are not yet Christ followers. It has long been my belief and practice to have vital relationships outside of normal church life. I truly believe that living a generous lifestyle has been my greatest platform to be a Christian witness. As a public speaker, I have not lacked in opportunities to present the gospel via spoken word. Could it be that what we do carries much more weight and influence than what we say?

If God's greatest act of generosity is measurable, how much more should our acts of generosity be measurable?

I once invited a friend, who is an unbeliever, to join me for a speaking engagement in Rome, Italy. It was during wintertime, and it was very cold and rainy. One afternoon, we were walking to a restaurant to have lunch with a pastor and some of his team members. As we approached the entrance, a homeless man sat shivering beside the door. What struck me was that he had no gloves, and his hands were bright red from the cold. Instinctively, I took off my gloves, leaned down, and put them into his hands. Without looking up, he took them and immediately put them on. As we continued into the restaurant, my friend said, "Brian, you know, you can't help everyone." I just smiled and said, "So true, but at least I could help him."

During the past twenty years, my friend has had a front row seat to observing my generosity journey. But this simple act of kindness on that wintry day in Rome may have been my single greatest witness to my good friend. One thing is for sure, people are watching our lives. It is my conviction that living a lifestyle of generosity for all the world to see is and can be our greatest witness. It is true that people don't care how much we know until they know how much we care. Authentic acts of generosity position us for God to work mightily through them. It has been said to always preach the gospel, and use words if necessary!

Neighborly Acts of Giving

Jamie and I have had a clear sense that God was leading us to every place we have lived. There are countless stories to be told, but I will highlight only a few that seem to stand out. It should be reiterated that goals for generosity should include gifts of our time, talent, and treasure. In the sphere of doing everyday life, the goal should be to make ourselves available as opportunities present themselves.

Neighbors have also had a front row seat at observing our lives. We had some very interesting neighbors living on both sides of us when we were youth pastors in Charlotte. On the one side was a rental property with tenants coming and going on a regular basis, but on the other side lived a longtime resident. The longtime resident was neither very friendly nor interested in making small talk. One night, a terrible storm came through our neighborhood. My long-term neighbor had several huge oak trees on his property, and one of the massive ones fell across the fence dividing our yards. The next morning, I called a friend who was very experienced with a chain saw and tree removal. He came immediately and began cutting the portion of the tree that had fallen in my yard. As he cut the tree, I began to remove the debris.

The neighbor heard the commotion and came out to see what we were doing. He went back inside but would occasionally look out his window to observe our progress. Once we finished in my yard, I knocked on the neighbor's door and asked if he would like us to clear his yard as well. He abruptly replied, "Well, how much is that gonna cost me?" I replied, "Well, nothing, sir. This is what neighbors do for each other in times like this." My friend proceeded to cut up the tree, and my neighbor and I removed all the debris. It took almost all day to finish the work.

By the end of the day, I had made a new friend in my neighbor. This simple act of generosity dramatically changed his attitude toward me and my young family. He knew that I worked at a church, but never seemed impressed. I came to realize that acts of generosity could become a solid platform to be a witness in the marketplace.

Authentic acts of generosity position us
for God to work mightily through them.

A year or so later, a second-hand vehicle I bought had a blown head gasket. It was going to be costly to repair, as it was labor intensive. I asked the same neighbor if he knew of a reliable garage for me to take it. He replied, "I sure do," and with a smile, he returned to his house. About an hour later, there was a knock at my door. It was my neighbor with his adult son, who just happened to be a mechanic. The car repair only cost me about ten dollars (the cost of the part) and a few glasses of iced tea. When I asked that he please let me pay his son for his time, he chimed, "No, sir, this is what neighbors do for each other in times like this." It is so much more humbling to receive than it is to give.

The house we moved into after I became the lead pastor in Charlotte was in a beautiful neighborhood. After living there a short time, an African American family moved next door. When we went over to introduce ourselves, my neighbor made it clear that they expected to be shunned because they were the only people of color in the neighborhood. We told him we couldn't speak for anyone else but that being neighbors had nothing to do with skin color. A short time later, his wife had to have surgery. Jamie made a cake, and we took it over to them. The man stood there in amazement that we would do such an act of kindness. He mentioned never being treated well by any white people. Again, I said, "This is what neighbors do for each other." Their kids played with our kids. Their children came to church with our girls on several occasions. He also had a special gift for making BBQ ribs on his grill. I was the recipient of those wonderful ribs many times. But it all started with a single act of generosity.

God Sent Jamie to the One

Another example of a neighborly act of generosity is Jamie's story to tell. It is also the most powerful. We had always lived in a multi-level home, but we decided we needed to find a ranch style home—a one-story—as my knees were worsening due to old sports injuries. We found a perfect home to suit our needs in a great neighborhood. Jamie had a clear sense that God was preparing her for an assignment in our new neighborhood. Here is her story:

> When I agreed that we needed to find a home
> more suited to our needs, I struggled with leaving a
> neighborhood and neighbors that I loved. God was so

gracious to lead us to a lovely neighborhood less than two miles away from our previous home. On several occasions, I asked the Lord what the significance of this move was and if I had a particular assignment.

Our new home was under construction when we found it, and we often walked through it in the evenings after the construction workers were gone. It was during one of these walk-throughs that our soon-to-be neighbor, Laurence, came wandering into the home. Like Brian and I so often do, she loved to walk through homes as they were being built. After we exchanged introductions, I was so pleased to know that I had a next-door neighbor who was close to my age but very young at heart.

One afternoon, after we were settled in our new home, I was in the front yard as Laurence was pulling into her driveway. We stood outside and had a lengthy conversation where Laurence shared her story. What a story it was! In addition to being a cancer survivor, she had led an incredible life. I was so very intrigued by this new friend who was lovely, adventurous, and kind. As I started to return home, I heard these words in my spirit: "I have sent you to the one." I immediately knew what that meant. God was telling me that now, after years of serving as a pastor's wife and serving/leading in a larger capacity, my new assignment would be on an individual level.

Laurence had many close friends, several of whom I was fortunate to meet. She embodied the saying "To have a friend, you need to be a friend." When she wasn't off on one of her adventures, we enjoyed occasional coffee visits in each other's homes, attending a neighborhood Bible study, and taking walks together. But suddenly, Laurence began to get fatigued.

For several days, she didn't have the energy for our walks and finally made an appointment to see her doctor. We were devastated to find out that cancer had struck again. Our conversations became more focused on Scripture and relationship with Jesus. "I've sent you to the one" would be confirmed over and over again.

For weeks, Laurence went to the hospital for treatments. Her many friends cared for her during this time. There were times I drove her to her treatments, and we always prayed together before she left my car. Soon the treatments turned into hospital stays. During this time, I would water Laurence's plants, gather her mail, take her garbage bins to the curb, and keep an eye on her house, just as I had done when she was off on an adventure. I soon learned her preferences and schedules. I knew when I needed to unlock her front door for her house cleaners or when someone needed to be let in to install her new draperies. I loved how she never stopped planning or beautifying her home. It was never a burden to help where I could. Like Brian said, "It's what neighbors do."

After a few short months, Laurence went home to be with Jesus. In the days after her passing, I experienced such a mix of emotions. I missed her terribly but was so glad she was no longer suffering. I found myself becoming increasingly grateful that God had given me the privilege of having Laurence as a friend and neighbor. What a blessing it was! As cliché as it may sound, I believe she did more for me than I ever did for her. I'm reminded of a song that was sung in my home church during the '70s:

> Only one life, so soon it will pass.
> Only what's done for Christ will last.
> Only one chance to do His will,
> So give to Jesus all your days.
> It's the only life that pays
> When you recall you have but one life.
> [Lanny Wolfe]

Our time serving others is certainly time well spent, so be generous with your time. After all, it's what neighbors (Christ followers) do!

An Extraordinary Tip

I think it's also important to be generous toward those whose income depends on tips. I received a valuable lesson on tipping by observing a friend and mentor, Bishop Rick Thomas. We went to dinner one evening, and he valeted his car. Bishop pulled out a roll of twenty-dollar bills and seized the opportunity to make it a mentoring moment. He said, "Brian, I never tip less than $20." He believed that tipping placed a primary value upon the person and not the service they were providing. His example of generosity influenced me profoundly. In fact, it is not uncommon for me to receive a notice from my credit card company requesting verification of a tip. The notice usually states, "Did you intend to give the [$$$] tip amount? This is an extraordinary tip." I must admit, it is a badge of honor to receive this kind of notice.

Bishop Rick was also instrumental in helping me define my message. He asked me one day many years ago, "Brian, what is your message?" Confused by the question, I muttered some response. He kept prodding me, "What is your message?" I confessed, "I don't know!" Ultimately, that simple question would lead to the self-discovery that my lane—my core message—was generosity. It put me on the path that I am now pursuing. The passion of my message is to inspire you as you pursue your own generosity journey!

Chapter 9 Takeaway

Take a moment to think and pray about setting a goal of increasing your giving, whether it be of your time, talents, or treasure. God has placed people, churches, or ministries around you where you can practice becoming more generous. Perhaps you have a story of when you have given to someone or when someone has given to you. Reflect on that. If you don't have a story, then what do you feel God leading you to do? Be encouraged to step into it today. You will never regret it!

CHAPTER 10 THE STORM

*"The godly will flourish like a palm tree; they will
grow strong like the cedars of Lebanon."*
Psalm 92:12

In early 2020, the ominous COVID cloud began settling upon our world. This chapter was not a part of the original outline or manuscript; however, I decided to include it as it became extremely relevant to our personal generosity journey. Further, it seemed relevant, given the fact that COVID has impacted and changed society as a whole in an unprecedented capacity. Little could any of us have known the societal trauma that would be forced upon us by this indiscriminate virus. We all have a story to tell. This is ours!

Two significant things happened to Jamie and me in the first few weeks of the COVID shutdown. About 25 percent of our income stream comes from my weekend speaking engagements. For thirty years, I had spoken almost every Sunday. When I moved into a hybrid missions role, my goal was to travel and speak about two weekends a month. So we established our schedule and budget accordingly. In March 2020, my schedule for the year was comfortably full with weekend services and several international trips. I was scheduled to speak in Binghamton, New York, at two separate churches, one on Thursday, March 26 and the other on Sunday March 29. These became my first cancellation casualties. Over the next few weeks, everything on my calendar would cancel for the next six months.

It bears repeating: Faith never gets any easier!

I keenly recall sitting in the living room with Jamie on the morning of April 1. I wondered if this could all be a cruel April Fools' prank. We discussed our new reality and how for the foreseeable future, we would be facing a 25 percent budget shortfall. Initially, we projected it would be four months of no income stream from weekend travel. It turned into a full six months. Several weeks prior, we had attended a Kingdom Builders missions banquet at our home church. We made a sizable faith promise for the coming year. This became a central part of our budgetary discussion.

We had a large missions offering in hand, all the while facing a looming deficit in our finances. In that moment of decision, we drew from everything we have shared with you in this book. Even though we were facing one of the greatest financial challenges of our life, we decided we were not going to change our priorities; we would stay the course. It bears repeating: Faith never gets any easier! Those were sobering moments for us as we prayed, set our course, and asked the Lord to see us through this storm. Of course, we had no idea of its size and scope.

On Friday, April 3, I went online and gave our Kingdom Builders missions faith promise offering. The following Monday,

I received a call from a pastor. After a few minutes of chatting, he said, "God spoke to me to send you a check." Mind you, I hadn't been scheduled to speak at this church, so there was no "reason" for this gift. The check arrived in the mail a few days later. Up to that point in our missions ministry, this was the largest gift we had ever received. That check covered the first four months of our budget shortfall. Psalm 37:18–19 became oh so real:

> Day by day the LORD takes care of the innocent, and
> they will receive an inheritance that lasts forever.
> They will not be disgraced in hard times; **even in**
> **famine they will have more than enough.**

Over the next few months, I received a handful of similar phone calls. Each of those calls resulted in an unexpected monetary gift from a pastor saying, "God put you on our hearts to bless you!" With no exaggeration or embellishment, the amount from those gifts was more than double our projected budgetary shortfall. God is so good!

Mark's Perspective

The second significant thing occurred on Saturday, April 4. I posted a video blog sharing a word the Lord had given me early that morning regarding the COVID "storm." This word would eventually become a full message I titled "The Storm"—a message, I believe, has a prophetic edge with important relevance to Christ followers. Let's start with Mark 6:

Immediately after this, Jesus **insisted** that his disciples get back into the boat and head across the lake to Bethsaida, while he sent the people home. After telling everyone good-bye, he went up into the hills by himself to pray.

Late that night, the disciples were in their boat in the middle of the lake, and Jesus was alone on land. He saw that they were in **serious trouble**, rowing hard and struggling against the wind and waves. About three o'clock in the morning Jesus came toward them, walking on the water. **He intended to go past them**, but when they saw him walking on the water, they cried out in terror, thinking he was a ghost. They were all terrified when they saw him.

But Jesus spoke to them at once. "Don't be afraid," he said. "Take courage! I am here!" Then he **climbed into the boat**, and the wind stopped. They were totally amazed, for they still **didn't understand** the significance of the miracle of the loaves. Their hearts were too hard to take it in.

Mark 6:45–52

A closer look at the story, when comparing it to the other Gospel accounts, is quite interesting. The following is a brief

Synoptic Gospel analysis of this fascinating story of Jesus sending His disciples into the storm:

- Gospel of Luke: Luke makes no mention of this story, as he was not an eyewitness.
- Gospel of Matthew: This is the only one of the four Gospels to mention Peter stepping out of the boat and walking toward Jesus. The only Gospel writers who were present and actual eyewitnesses were Matthew and John. But John makes no mention of Peter's exploits.
- Gospel of John: John only includes an abbreviated version of this story.
- Gospel of Mark: Mark offers an interesting and valuable perspective that the other three Gospels do not.

   He was of Roman descent and would have had to rely on second-hand information for this story. Some scholars estimate that 95 percent of Mark's Gospel is written from Peter's narrative. Therefore, in all likelihood, Mark was relying solely on Peter for his information, as he himself was not an eyewitness. I find it quite intriguing that there is no mention of Peter getting out of the boat and walking on the water in Mark's account. It is conjecture on my part, but one possibility could be that Peter chose to focus on the weightier aspects of the story.

   Additionally, only Mark's Gospel mentions that Jesus "intended to go past them" (v. 48) and that "they still didn't understand the significance of the miracle of the loaves. Their hearts were too hard to take it in" (v. 52).

I have heard many messages on Peter getting out of the boat or walking on the water or Jesus calming the storm. But in more than forty-five years as a Christ follower, I have never heard a message referencing Mark's unique perspective. Could it be that an overlooked aspect of this story is why the disciples were sent into the storm and the fact that it was Jesus' intent to "go past them"? My message, "The Storm," was birthed out of the conviction that Mark's perspective is an apropos metaphor for life during the COVID era and beyond. Let me offer three key takeaways to this story.

Jesus Sends Them into the Storm

> Immediately after this, Jesus **insisted** that his disciples get back into the boat and head across the lake to Bethsaida, while he sent the people home.
>
> Mark 6:45

The word "insisted" comes from the Greek word *anagkazo*, which means something is of necessity or as by authoritative command. The connotation is that Jesus, of necessity or as by an authoritative command, insisted that the disciples get into the boat, with full knowledge that He was sending them into a raging storm. Further, Jesus intended to rejoin His disciples on the other side of the lake. We know this because the text clearly states that He "intended to go past them" (v. 48). Jesus knew that even though there would be a fierce storm, they could make it through without His assistance. It is important to note that the storm is *never* the destination; it is merely a temporary obstacle to pass through!

In August 2018, I was in a hotel room in Warsaw, Poland, having a bit of a meltdown. Months prior, an opportunity had presented itself for me to enroll in a master's program in Missional Leadership at Trinity Graduate School. It was my held belief that such an opportunity was a prerequisite to writing this book. Earlier that day, I received an email with the syllabus attached for the first two classes. As I perused the class requirements, the chilling thought occurred to me that it had been over thirty-five years since I had finished my bachelor's degree. The said meltdown began to occur. I honestly did not think I was ready to take this challenge on. It appeared to be too daunting!

I immediately called Jamie. She was of course encouraging and understanding as she listened to me process. Finally, she calmly said, "Will you regret it if you don't at least attempt it?" This was a sobering thought. It was apparent to me that I was in for some misery either way. Then I called my good friend who had just completed his first year in the master's program. He offered me some tangible truths: "Listen, I know what you are in for, and I can coach you through it. Brian, you can do this." I chose my misery and decided to give it a go! Honestly, I felt like Jesus was sending me into a storm for which I was ill-prepared.

The storm is never the destination; it is merely a temporary obstacle to pass through!

From that memorable meltdown in Warsaw to the completion and release of *The Generosity Gene*, it has been a full four-year saga. The first two years were filled with learning how to write in an academic tone, reading hundreds of books and periodicals, writing countless papers and assignments, and attending in-class sessions. The last two years of the journey included prep work, outlining, writing the full manuscript, editing, publishing, etc. Keep in mind, all this was done while being technologically challenged in a techno world—and during the pandemic.

Throughout, it seemed like one crashing wave after another, a perpetual storm if you will! During this season, I heard someone say, "Your misery will become your ministry." I knew the Lord had sent me into my misery—the storm—but for a greater purpose. I had to routinely remind myself that the storm was not the destination. Rather, it was a temporary obstacle for me to pass through. As it turned out, I graduated with honors! To God be the Glory!

Jesus Climbs into the Storm

> About three o'clock in the morning Jesus came
> toward them, walking on the water. **He intended to
> go past them,** but when they saw him walking on
> the water, they cried out in terror, thinking he was a
> ghost. They were all terrified when they saw him. . . .
> **Then he climbed into the boat,** and the wind
> stopped.
>
> Mark 6:48–51

We can only speculate about why Jesus decided to climb
into the boat as opposed to continuing with His intent to go
past them. My speculation is that Jesus as Shepherd is quick to
respond to the cry of His sheep. Could it be that when we do
not have enough faith or strength to make it through our storm,
Jesus is there to respond to the cry of our hearts? I say yes to this
hypothesis. For most of us, our reality is that we don't pass every
test, and we don't necessarily handle every storm the way we
should. But Jesus is faithful to be there when we fail or fall short.
This should bring great comfort to our souls. In other words,
Jesus climbs into our storms!

There is a shopping mall about fifteen minutes from our
house, which has a train ride for children. Jamie and I took our
grandchildren Ella and Brody, who were about three years old at
that time, to ride the train. It moved at a pace that we could walk
alongside and be within arm's reach; however, Ella and Brody

insisted that Pop Pop get on the train with them. It was easy to see that they were scared to do it on their own. Well, as humbling and awkward as it would be, I somehow was able to wedge myself onto that train. It was a sight to see, for sure! Jamie just laughed and took pictures for posterity's sake.

In other words, Jesus climbs into our storms!

I was thankful the mall was not very full at the time. But as we rode along, I suddenly had an aha moment. I realized that this must be how it is for the Lord many times. He never leaves us and knows that we will be fine no matter our situations. But sometimes, we just need Him to climb into our situations, and the King of Glory does just that. He climbs into our boat, into our train, into our situations!

Jesus Makes Sense of the Storm

> Then he climbed into the boat, and the wind stopped. They were totally amazed, for they still didn't **understand** the significance of the miracle of the loaves. Their hearts were too hard to take it in.
>
> Mark 6:51–52

The Greek word for "understand," *syniemi*, means the collecting together of the individual features of an object into a whole, as collecting the pieces of a puzzle and putting them together. Notice the implication: All the puzzle pieces have to come together quickly for there to be a complete understanding of something that just happened. Apparently, the storm became a part of God's purpose to bring an understanding to the disciples that they were lacking.

It appears that the lessons to be learned from the feeding of the five thousand were not absorbed by the disciples. The verbiage "their hearts were too hard to take it in" (v. 52) is revealing. Seemingly, the purpose of the storm was to help them recalibrate. It worked! We have no record of what Jesus may have said to them once they reached the other side of the lake. We can only speculate. My thought is that He used it as an opportunity to recalibrate their faith and focus on Him!

The storm became a part of God's purpose to bring an understanding to the disciples that they were lacking.

Could it be that there are storms in our lives that God uses for a similar purpose? We may be in need of a recalibration of faith and focus. The stormy seasons of life are a perfect opportunity for our faith to grow stronger in Him!

Rooted Like a Palm Tree

As I began to develop my message "The Storm," I came across some interesting information regarding the palm tree, like the ones found in Psalm 92:12–13:

But the godly will **flourish** like palm trees and
grow strong like the cedars of Lebanon. For they
are transplanted to the LORD's own house. They
flourish in the courts of our God.

Even when I went to college in Florida, where palm trees are
quite common, I had never given the tree much thought. But as
I was researching the palm trees referenced in Psalm 92, I found
some interesting information. First of all, the connotation of the
word "flourish" in the original Hebrew is to grow or develop in a
healthy or vigorous way, especially as the result of a particularly
favorable environment. However, the most interesting
information I found was that the most favorable environment for
a palm tree's growth is a storm.

The storm is similar to how *using* our muscles actually makes
them stronger. When palm trees are blown and buffeted during
heavy storms, their roots grow deeper and stronger—so deep and
so strong, in fact, that when the high winds come, palm trees can
bend almost in half, but they rarely fall down.

Read the first part of that verse again: "But the godly will
flourish like palm trees." Scripture assures you that you will
flourish—or grow and develop as a result of your environment.
You can trust God to both provide and allow the most "favorable"
environment for your growth to happen.

I stated from the very beginning of the COVID storm that the Lord would not only see us through it but would also help us to somehow make sense of it. The coronavirus pandemic is the equivalent of a world-wide hurricane force wind severely beating down on all aspects of society. But you, my friend, are like a palm tree stretching and growing stronger amidst the pandemic storm. You will both flourish and thrive as a result of this storm. It is impossible to see the root structure of the palm tree, just as it is impossible to see the faith root system in your life. Nevertheless, you have been designed by your Creator, similar to the palm tree, to ultimately flourish through the storm.

The real issue is not if there will be storms in life. Rather, the real issue becomes how you decide to react during the storm and what you plan to do differently after the storm. As for me and my house, we choose to trust the Lord!

Chapter 10 Takeaway

I want you to know that the storm you may be in right now is not your destination. However, the lesson God wants you to learn through it is! Has there been a time in your life where a storm came, and you started to feel the necessities of life trying to block your generosity? What happened, and in what ways might you change your response next time, knowing that Jesus is with you in the midst of it?

CHAPTER 11   THE GATEKEEPERS

*"Stand at the gate of the L*ORD*'s house and there proclaim this message: 'Hear the word of the Lord, all you people of Judah who come through these gates to worship the L*ORD*.'"*
Jeremiah 7:2 NIV

I am writing this chapter primarily for pastors who are the spiritual gatekeepers for their congregations and communities. Pastors, you too need to be inspired and encouraged in your personal generosity journeys as you lead your people into greater realms of generosity.

In biblical times, the main gate to a city was a place for commerce, judicial activities, for kings to pass down edicts, and for the prophets to proclaim their messages. Additionally, the main gate was a place where the Word of God was read openly to the people. It is very apparent that whoever controlled the gates controlled the city. Therefore, a gatekeeper served in a very strategic position and affected anyone entering or exiting the city.

The gatekeepers of the temple determined all access and activities germane to the temple. In modern times, pastors are the primary spiritual gatekeepers to and for the church. Even though I no longer pastor a church, I am still a pastor at heart. I think like a pastor, have the heart and perspective of a shepherd, and understand the umpteen challenges facing pastors in this chaotic world.

Coach Bill McCartney won a national championship as the head coach of the University of Colorado in 1990. In that same year, he founded the incredible men's movement known as Promise Keepers. I once heard Coach McCartney make a statement that has served me well throughout much of my ministry. He said, "The greatest form of motivation is encouragement." I am an avid believer in this mindset. In my travels as a guest speaker, I have the privilege of interfacing with a myriad of pastor-gatekeepers, and my goal is to always be a source of personal encouragement to them. The more a pastor is built up and encouraged, the greater chance that encouragement will flow into church leadership and thus into the entire church body.

Gateway Churches

I remember driving into Hickory, North Carolina, for the first time when we were considering a move there. A sign just outside the city captured my attention: "Hickory, Gateway to Northwestern North Carolina." Hickory is known as a gateway city. In that moment, the Holy Spirit nudged my heart that the church of which we were considering becoming the lead pastors was a gateway church. Sometimes, as pastors, we may underestimate or undervalue the spiritual significance of the people and places to which God calls us. As for me, I had an awareness that the activities that took place at the church could have important spiritual implications in the community and the entire region.

During the early stages of putting this book together, I had an unexpected encounter with a close friend of mine, Teo. He and his family were part of the church we used to pastor in Hickory. Due to a family tragedy they had experienced, Jamie and I traveled back to Hickory to spend a few days with them. While visiting, I was fascinated to hear the in-depth story of how they had immigrated from Romania. I share this generosity journey as an aside, just to inspire you.

At the age of twenty-eight, Teo fled communist Romania by crossing the Danube River on a rubber raft in the dark of night. After five months in an internment camp, he was finally selected to emigrate to the United States. He arrived in Fort Lauderdale, Florida, unable to speak any English, and with less than a dollar in his pocket. Teo was able to secure work with an electrical contractor for five dollars an hour and, through much perseverance, learned English. All the while, his wife and their son and daughter had to remain in Romania. After a few years, they were reunited and eventually found their way to our church in Hickory.

The more a pastor is built up and encouraged, the greater chance that encouragement will flow.

By the time they started attending our church, they had two other children and had been in the United States for almost twenty years. They were doing well for themselves, as Teo now owned his own electrical company and had a general contractor license, and Michelle had become a nurse. But there was more to their story.

One afternoon, during our visit, Teo and I were sitting on his back porch when he looked at me with tears and said, "The first time I ever heard a message on tithing and giving was from you. Your teaching changed our lives." I must admit, I was caught off guard by his comment. More importantly, I was shocked to hear that in his entire life as a believer, he had never heard a pastor teach on the biblical principle of the tithe. He went on to say, "There is no telling how much further we would be in our generosity journey had we been taught the tithing principle twenty years earlier."

The Tithe Talk

God's great blessing is upon us all when we give, and I personally believe that the tithe should be considered a starting point in giving, even under the new covenant of grace. I fully understand and appreciate that there are multiple theological vantage points regarding the tithe. For example, I recently had a discussion with a doctoral seminary student who shared with me that the tithe is under the old covenant law and is, therefore, irrelevant, as Jesus had fulfilled the law. My response was that even in the new covenant of grace, since God's grace and generosity cannot be separated, the tithe should be considered a standard for giving.

In fact, by all appearances, the early earmarks of new covenant generosity far exceeded old covenant standards. Let's take a look at what transpired in the New Testament church in Acts 4:32–35, where generosity can easily be seen as a vital core value to the early church:

> All the believers were united in heart and mind. And they felt that what they owned was not their own, so they shared **everything** they had. The apostles testified powerfully to the resurrection of the Lord Jesus, and God's great blessing was upon them all. There were **no needy people** among them, because those who owned land or houses would sell them and bring the money to the apostles **to give** to those in need.

As has been stated, my goal is to encourage pastors in all things related to generosity. For Jamie and me, we came to a heart decision that tithing would be the foundational piece in both our personal and pastoral generosity journeys. Once we settled this matter in our hearts, we have never looked back. As I mentioned in chapter 9, there is only one place in Scripture where God issues a challenge to put Him "to the test."

I will open the windows of heaven for you. I will
pour out a blessing so great you won't have enough
room to take it in! Try it! Put me to the test!

Malachi 3:10

I can assure you that we have never regretted our decision to
trust the Lord with the tithe! Further, we made it a key part of
our discipleship training during our pastoral ministry. We have
also never regretted our decision to make it a core value in our
ministry paradigm.

The tithe should be considered
a starting point in giving.

During my research, I must admit how surprised I was to
discover that a high percentage of gatekeepers—pastors—appear
to be reluctant to teach on the biblical precepts of giving. At
some point during that research, I came across an article in
Christianity Today, written by Rob Moll. I don't recall the exact
words, but he said something to the effect of, "A study found that
a major reason Christians do not give is because they are not
asked to." He said that researchers found "a strong correlation
between perceived expectations and readiness to give money."
He explained that most denominations believe Christians
should give 10 percent of their incomes, "but this teaching is
rarely reinforced."

It would be pure speculation on my part as to the myriad of reasons why gatekeepers would choose not to ask or reinforce scriptural teachings on giving. My purpose is neither to evaluate nor to speculate on the motives of pastors. Rather, it is my desire to encourage and educate pastors on the incredible importance and value of teaching generosity to their people. My hope is that this book will inspire many more gatekeepers to do so.

Reasons to Teach on Giving

I believe that there are three primary reasons pastors shy away from or avoid speaking on giving altogether. The first is to avoid any association with some extreme generosity teachings found in the body of Christ. The key word here is "extreme." If the goal and motivation of giving centers on receiving in such a way that a lavish lifestyle is the end game, this would be considered extreme. Pure and simple, the goal of generosity becomes *me* centric. In other words, the purpose of giving is to receive a blessing to hoard. This mindset leads to a reservoir mentality, where the harvest of blessing is stored up, as opposed to being a conduit or tributary of blessing that consistently flows through our lives.

As has been established in previous chapters, sowing seed with the expectation of a return harvest is a biblical principle. However, when this principle takes on an extreme dimension and selfish motives get involved, the truth can easily be distorted. In large part, it is the responsibility of the gatekeepers to teach a balanced gospel that keeps self-serving tendencies in check.

I believe wholeheartedly that God wants to bless us to be a blessing. Being blessed financially is a beautiful thing when the goal is reaching the lost at any cost!

Let's take God at His word to put Him to the test!

The second reason pastors may avoid teaching on giving is that it can appear to be self-serving. Admittedly, this is a very real concern for many pastors. In some cases, a pastor's salary may be directly related to the income algorithms of the church finances. A pastor may have incentive clauses in his salary package. Therefore, some pastors may shy away from teaching on giving to protect themselves from being labeled as selfish or greedy. Understand, a pastor's motives can be very sincere and pure. But the fact remains that pastors have the spiritual responsibility to teach biblical generosity, all the while guarding themselves against impure motives. It could be that if a pastor has become self-serving, it will be evident in multiple areas of his or her life and ministry. On the other hand, if a pastor strives to keep "self" in check, it will also be evident in other areas of life and ministry.

The third reason pastors may avoid stewardship teaching is the likelihood of some negative reactions by parishioners. I will refrain from sharing the plethora of reactions I have personally experienced during my pastorates. But make no mistake, this is a reality for which gatekeepers must accept and be prepared. Further, pastors may fear people leaving the church because giving is being taught. I have always believed that you tend to attract people based upon who you are, which is reflected in what you teach. If you lose people because you are teaching biblical generosity, then so be it. On the other hand, there is a high likelihood that you will also attract countless others who fully embrace a balanced and biblically based teaching on generosity!

As gatekeepers, pastors are tasked with the spiritual responsibility to address these glaring inequities among believers in their churches. I believe we do a disservice to our people when we either remain silent or skirt the issue of biblical stewardship. Again, it is not my intent to evaluate and monitor the motives of pastors. I only encourage that pastors have motives that benefit the spiritual welfare of the flock God has entrusted to them. That includes encouraging God's people to grow and prosper in their generosity journey. Let's take God at His word to put Him to the test!

The Flint, the Honeycomb, and the Sponge

Many times, when I am speaking on my favorite topic of generosity and a missions offering ensues, I use an illustration of three types of givers: the flint, the honeycomb, and the sponge. Approximately 10 percent of people are flint givers. To get them to give anything, you must hammer it, and then you only get bits and pieces. Another 10 percent of people are honeycomb givers. A honeycomb overflows out of its own sweetness. Pastors love honeycomb givers! But the other 80 percent of people are sponge givers. The idea of the sponge is that the more you squeeze, the more you get! In a lighthearted way, I let them know that I am about to put the squeeze on them for a missions offering.

Could it be that these believers are stuck in their spiritual walk and experiencing stress because they have not progressed in their generosity journey?

The idea of squeezing may make some uncomfortable. This is surely not my intent. However, it is a suitable metaphor if understood and applied responsibly. My putting the squeeze on people is the equivalent of asking them to give. As has been established, the vast majority of church attendees are *expecting* to be asked. The pastor is tasked with the stewardship for both teaching and asking, but when applied lovingly and carefully, the sheep will respond and grow spiritually as a result. I do not believe in manipulating or coercing people. But I do believe that people should be provided with regular and consistent opportunities to generously support the work of God going forth.

Why All Believers Should Give

It's important to give attention to the responsibility that all believers have as the gatekeepers for their own lives. In chapter 3, I alluded to the many reasons people get stuck on their spiritual journey. At some point, honest evaluation and assessment is necessary. Many times, they are stuck because of financial stress. Could it be that these believers are stuck in their spiritual walk and experiencing stress because they have not progressed in their generosity journey?

If this hits close to home, please allow me to encourage you. From my pastoral experience, when people have stagnated in their walk with the Lord, they either make excuses for their stagnation or try to pass on the blame to others. This does not solve the problem of being stuck. Here is the beauty of God's plan: The moment you take ownership and accept responsibility as the gatekeeper of your own life and begin to apply biblical principles to your situation, you will once again begin to make spiritual progress. As it relates to your generosity journey, when you honor the Lord in your giving, you will get "unstuck."

Another telling Scripture is found in Matthew 6:21, which says, "Wherever your treasure is, there the desires of your heart will also be." As it relates to generosity, it is ultimately a heart issue. As we have already established, the heart regulates the hands. If your treasure is founded in your stuff, you will hold too tightly to it and struggle to give any of it away. However, if your treasure is founded first in the Lord and His harvest, you will hold more loosely to it. The bottom line is that you are the gatekeeper of your treasure. When Jesus is the Lord of your life and your value system, your priorities will reflect it!

---

*If your treasure is founded first in the Lord,
you will hold more loosely to it.*

Finally, let me remind you of one simple, yet profound truth. God wants to bless you to be a blessing to countless others. As you have read throughout the pages of this book, there are no shortcuts. When you are willing to sow the stuff of your life, God always has a harvest in mind. When the stuff of your life is sown into rich gospel soil, it has the potential to reach people around the globe for Christ. Only heaven will reveal the full impact of your faithful generosity, but you can expect harvest seasons in your life on this side of heaven as well. I can promise you that God keeps an accurate log of the generosity of your time, talent, and treasure!

A Prayer for Pastors as Spiritual Gatekeepers

Lord, I lift up all the men and women who are called by Your name to serve Your people as spiritual gatekeepers, as well as the emerging generation of gatekeepers now preparing for full-time service. May there be a fresh anointing of the Holy Spirt to empower them. May they begin to experience a renewed courage to boldly proclaim the Word of God in an uncompromising manner. May an overwhelming spirit of generosity be theirs in Christ Jesus. May that same spirit of generosity flow to their leadership teams as well as throughout their entire congregations. May there be a tangible presence of God that permeates the entire church body they serve. May acts of generosity toward their communities be received as an authentic Christian witness. And may there be new levels of global missions awareness released in their lives and ministries. In Jesus' name. Amen!

Chapter 11 Takeaway

As a pastor of a local church, you have been made to be a spiritual gatekeeper to help your congregation grow in generosity. After reading this chapter, have you identified areas wherein you need to grow or develop? What are they? Be courageous, Pastor, in your efforts to challenge your people to grow in generosity.

As a believer, you have been made to be a gatekeeper for your own life. After reading this chapter, what are the areas of generosity that need to grow or develop in you? Maybe the Lord is challenging you in a specific area of your life. I want to encourage you to step into new realms of generosity as the Holy Spirit leads you!

CHAPTER 12   THE FINISH

"Now finish the work, so that your eager willingness to do it may be matched by your completion of it, according to your means."
2 Corinthians 8:11 NIV

Several years ago, Jamie and I visited our missionary friends, Rick and Jennifer Pasquale, in Rome. They were gracious to be our tour guides during our stay, which included touring the Vatican and Saint Peter's Basilica. The history, the opulence, the artistry, the ornate décor, and the sheer size were all a sight to behold. However, for me personally, it was not a spiritually empowering experience. Later that same day, we happened to be randomly walking down a side street in Rome when we noticed a small sign that read, "The Apostle Luke's Home." There was no line for entry or any fanfare whatsoever (in contrast, we had stood in line at Saint Peter's Basilica for over an hour). The apostle Paul had stayed with Luke in the latter days of his life and ministry all while being under house arrest. I must admit that I was not prepared for the overwhelming impact of this impromptu visit. It was in fact a God moment!

As we toured the home, we noticed Scripture readings on the wall written by Paul in his second letter to Timothy during his house imprisonment. As we entered the small, dug out basement area, we saw a Bible verse framed on the wall, which said, "I have fought the good fight, I have finished the race, I have kept the faith" (see 2 Tim. 4:7). Displayed on another wall in the same room was, "Only Luke is with me" (see 2 Tim. 4:11). I was overcome with emotion as the gravity of these words gripped my heart. These were very precious and special moments that Jamie and I shared together that day. Little could we have known that these two verses would later become the framework and mandate for the rest of our life in ministry.

Paul offered an admonition to the church at Corinth: "Now **finish the work,** so that your eager willingness to do it may be matched by your completion of it, according to your means" (2 Cor. 8:11 NIV). The word "finish" comes from the Greek word *epiteleo*, which means not only to be willing but also to press on to action. The implication is that it is not enough to be willing or have good intentions. Rather, there is an absolute call to action! Scripture refers to being more than a hearer of the Word but a doer of the *work* (see James 1:25). For me, the inference is clear that we are to finish the work before we finish the race. We all have a work to do as believers. This definitely includes generosity!

The Iron Man

Scott Rigsby is a motivational speaker whom I invited to speak at our church during my last pastorate. He had been in a horrendous accident as a young man and lost both legs just above the knees. For years, he struggled terribly with his newfound identity. With the help of the Lord, Scott eventually found his way through the maze of emotions and challenges and decided he would begin to train for an Ironman triathlon race. The Ironman triathlon is made up of a 2.4-mile swim, 112-mile bike ride, and a 26.2-mile run.

Scott tells the story of his multiple mishaps and challenges during those first few races. Consequently, he was unable to finish the early ones. But he continued to train incessantly for years with one goal in mind: to finish a race! He was once asked by a reporter which part of the race was his favorite. The reporter must have been thinking Scott's answer would be either the swim, the bike ride, or the run. Scott's reply was "The finish!"

When Scott finally reached his first finish line, it was long after all the other competitors had finished. There were virtually no onlookers left. Still, it must have been an incredible moment of overwhelming emotion and pure satisfaction as he crossed the finish line. It reminds me of Paul's words to Timothy: "Only Luke is with me!"

We are to finish the work before we finish the race. This definitely includes generosity.

It is hard to grasp that the man who wrote most of the New Testament epistles and is inarguably one of the most influential people in all of Christianity came to the end of his journey with only Luke by his side. A perspective we should consider is that the greatest rewards for the believer are stored up in heaven to be enjoyed for eternity. The goal must be to finish the work of our calling no matter how lonely or thankless it may be at times.

Scott Rigsby was finally able to complete an ironman triathlon due to the tireless effort he put forth to properly train for many years. Plus, he never gave up or quit! There were no shortcuts. Because he put in the necessary work, he was able to finish the race. The same principle is applicable to our spiritual lives. God has a work and a calling for every believer. I believe that our ultimate reward directly relates to how we embrace and apply ourselves to our individual calling. And I believe that generosity is a key part of the work to which God has called us.

Ruined for the Ordinary

God's calling on some is to become missionaries, those who leave everything familiar to settle on foreign soil for the sake of the gospel. In my extensive travels, I have had the great privilege to meet many of these wonderful servants of God serving in foreign lands. Typically, there are two common requests every missionary has: First and foremost, they always ask for prayer! Second, they ask for resources or additional funding to facilitate the vision God has given them. Most missionaries are required to raise their own financial support from churches, family, and friends. But once they get to their assigned country, a myriad of additional needs arise that require finances.

There is a divine partnership between missionaries or missions organizations and faithful supporters operating in their generosity gene. The takeaway is that taking the gospel to all the world requires a mammoth number of resources. I stand by my favorite appeal when asking for missions dollars: Everyone can do some, some can do more, and a few can do much!

A thought I try to convey to both individuals as well as churches is that "God has not called you to reach the whole world, but He has called you to reach a portion of it." There should be some people group, project, or country of the world that God has laid on your heart. If not, pray and ask Him to do so. Consequently, what might you be willing to sacrificially give toward the needs of these people? Friend, this is a key part of the work to which God has called all of us. In addition, there may be some creative ways to apply your time and talents as well. If possible, I encourage you to visit the place and people who have captured your heart. It will change your life! Quite possibly, it will ruin you for the ordinary.

They Never Saw Their Greatest Harvest

As has been stated repeatedly throughout the pages of this book, my deep desire is to inspire you to greater depths of generosity. In part, I have used the power of story to do so. Let me offer three powerful examples that have impacted my life significantly. Each one had a unique calling and work they were called to do. The common denominator from each story is that they completed their work but never got to see the harvest. As it relates to generosity, I believe this is a very important perspective!

God has not called you to reach the whole world, but He has called you to reach a portion of it.

In August 1964, J. W. Tucker and his family were leaving to return to the Congo for their fifth four-year term as long-term missionaries. They had been in the States for a year raising much-needed financial support. Less than a week after returning, their village was captured by rebels, and the Tuckers were cut off from all communication to the outside world. When paratroopers landed in the Congo to stop the rebels, the rebels began to retaliate with killings, beatings, and torture. Tucker was taken captive by the rebels and savagely beaten to death one day before paratroopers arrived in Paulis to rescue him.

Tucker is the first and only Assemblies of God foreign missionary to be killed for the sake of the gospel. After his death, the rebels had put his body, along with several others, in the back of a truck and drove approximately sixty-five kilometers to dump them into the Bomokandi River. No one knows exactly why they made that drive to dispose of the bodies, but we assume they wanted to destroy the evidence. The bodies were never found, as they were thrown off a bridge into the river. It was presumed they were eaten by crocodiles.

The people who live in the area near the Bomokandi River are called the Mangbetu. Months later, when the rebellion began calming down, an army colonel who had been led to Christ by Tucker returned to the Mangbetu region. This colonel went to share the gospel with the people who had never heard it before, but he was rejected. Then the colonel discovered an ancient tribal belief held by the Mangbetu people, which basically says, "If a man's blood flows in the Bomokandi river, you are obligated to hear his message." He went back to the Mangbetu people and reminded them of this statute. The colonel said J. W. Tucker's blood flowed in the waters, so they must hear his message.

As a result of J. W. Tucker's body being thrown in the Bomokandi River, the message of the gospel was preached. Today, in the region where the river flows among the many tiny villages of the Mangbetu people, there are no fewer than sixty-six established churches. You see, J. W. Tucker sacrificed his own life for the sake of the gospel. Therefore, he never got to see the greatest harvest of his life!

Victor Plymire departed the United States in 1908 to settle in northwest China as a missionary. During those early years, he learned the language and culture, established relationships, shared the gospel, provided limited medical services, and did whatever else his hand found to do. He and his wife, Grace, lived and worked in extremely difficult conditions. In 1924, after almost sixteen years of faithful ministry, they finally had their first convert to Christ.

One of the major health threats in China during the 1920s was smallpox. As the epidemic swept through the region in which the Plymires were living, Grace and their son John both fell ill. Victor nursed them both and asked God to spare their lives. Sadly, John died on January 20, 1927, and Grace died a week later. Victor was unable to bury his wife and son in the public cemetery due to local superstitions about foreigners. Instead, he bought a small piece of land on a hillside outside the city as a burial site. Victor decided to deed the land to the church that he had planted there, which would become consequential many years later.

In the months prior to the death of his wife and son, Victor had been planning an extensive 2,000-mile trek across Tibet and into India. God had given him a vision to share the Good News with people who had never heard the gospel. Despite his grief over losing his family, he continued forward with planning for this journey. On May 18, 1927, Victor launched the 2,000-mile expedition, along with five companions and forty-seven beasts of burden carrying supplies. The group trekked through mountain passes, navigating some of the world's highest peaks and faced blizzards, avalanches, bandits, and hostile people. Along the eleven-month journey, almost all on horseback, his small expedition distributed 74,000 Gospels of John and approximately 40,000 gospel tracts in the Mongolian and Tibetan language.

The trip concluded in Calcutta, India, on February 28, 1928. Victor had been entirely cut off from communication with the West, and his family and supporters presumed him dead. When he sailed back to China in 1928, he met a man with a copy of an Assemblies of God publication, which contained a notice of his death. Over the years, he joked that he was one of the few people who had a chance to read his own obituary. Victor remarried and had two more children. He continued to serve in China until 1949 when he was forced to leave due to the communist revolution. Consequently, China would be closed off to the West for the next twenty-five years. Victor died on December 8, 1956, never having seen the fruit and harvest of his labors, particularly from the 2,000-mile trek through Tibet to share the gospel.

Under communist rule in China, all personal properties were seized by the government. This included the land on which Grace and John were buried. However, because Victor had the presence of mind to deed the property to the church, the land was restored to the church sixty-seven years later. God used the gravesite to restore the church property to His people. During the twenty-five-year communication blackout in China, it would be discovered that God had been doing a special work from the seed of the 74,000 Gospels distributed. Thousands of churches had been birthed, and there was a thriving underground network that could be easily traced to the ministry of Victor Plymire. He finished the work and his race on earth without ever seeing the harvest!

Around the time China began to reopen to the West, there was a great revival taking place in Brazil. During this revival, God gave missionary Don Stamps an assignment to produce a comprehensive study Bible. The new converts coming to Christ as a result of the revival far exceeded the church's capacity to provide pastors for them. This, too, created unique challenges, as brand-new believers with a leadership gifting were becoming pastors with little or no training. In many cases, sound biblical doctrine took a backseat to the experiential. Stamps believed the solution to this challenge was a proper study Bible in their heart language.

It took Don Stamps and a team of Bible scholars almost ten years to complete this task. Every single word of the study notes was handwritten by Stamps. His wife, Linda, typed all the notes on an old manual typewriter. During the latter stages of finishing the study notes, Don was diagnosed with stomach cancer. He suffered terribly but continued the work. It was said that in the final few months of completing the Bible, he no longer asked for healing; he only prayed for more time to finish the work. God answered his prayer. The day Linda finished typing the notes, Don died of cancer at fifty-three years of age. You see, Stamps never got to see the harvest of his study Bible, which was first known as *The Life in the Spirit Study Bible*. It later changed to *The Full Life Study Bible*.

In the early 1990s, a small group of pastors decided to partner with Life Publishers in Springfield, Missouri. They had a heartfelt vision to see Stamps's study Bible translated into the top one hundred languages of the world. The first translation would be Chinese. Somehow, the name *Fire Bible* emerged during this process. That very first Chinese translation became known as *The Chinese Fire Bible*. The goal was to print and distribute one million of them to the underground churches in China. In all, over three million *Chinese Fire Bibles* were printed and distributed.

Living for the Harvest

It was an impactful moment for me when I came to the realization that the unseen harvests of Victor Plymire and Don Stamps had ultimately intersected. The seed of Plymire's 2,000-mile trek across Tibet would serve as the origin of the underground churches in China. The seed of Don Stamps's work became a vital resource to these same underground churches with a world-class study Bible. What a marvelous thing!

Fast forward with me to the time of writing this book. The *Fire Bible* has currently been translated into sixty-four different languages, with over eleven million copies distributed worldwide. We have another eight translations due to be completed by the end of 2022 or early 2023. I say "we" because I get the privilege of laboring in Don Stamps's vineyard as an ambassador for the *Fire Bible*. Each copy is an expensive undertaking. Many of my speaking engagements coincide with doing fundraising for our *Fire Bible* translations. Presently, this is a significant part of the work God has called me to do.

The greatest harvest of our lives will outlive us.

The real-life stories of J. W. Tucker, Victor Plymire, and Don Stamps remind me of another true story regarding coach Herb Brooks and the 1980 USA Olympic Hockey team. Many years after they won the gold medal as heavy underdogs, a movie called *The Miracle* was made to commemorate their achievement. It is a very inspiring story of how success is possible when hard work and teamwork blend to perfection. At the conclusion of the film, an update is given on each of the players on that winning roster. The final update is about Coach Herb Brooks. The caption reads, "This film is dedicated to the memory of Herb Brooks, who died shortly following principal photography. He never saw it. He lived it." The same could be said of missionaries Tucker, Plymire, and Stamps! They never saw it! They lived it!

It is important to live life in view of eternity. There will be the occasional harvest we get to experience on this side of heaven. It is wonderful when this happens, and it should be enjoyed to the fullest. Likely, the greatest harvest of our lives will outlive us all. This seems to be the way God intended it to be.

Chapter 11 of the Book of Hebrews is known as "The Faith Hall of Fame." It records the many exploits of the heroes who have gone before us. In the final two verses in the chapter, it is said of them, "All these people earned a good reputation because of their faith, yet none of them received all that God had promised. For God had something better in mind for us, so that they would not reach perfection without us" (Heb. 11:39–40).

Let us, therefore, live, give, and serve with a similar expectation as these faith heroes!

Pass the Baton

I stated in the introduction that I carry a keen sense of responsibility to the forthcoming generations, which includes my children, grandchildren, and beyond. My philosophy is simple: I still believe in heroes. Spiritual heroes are those who have lived in such a way that they left a mark, a legacy if you will. I am indebted to those who have impacted my life for the ordinary, especially as it relates to generosity. My personal heroes of faith have been mentioned throughout the pages of this book. Is it possible that the most powerful way to pass the baton to emerging generations is through the power of stories of living epistles? Could it be this simple? I say yes!

You now know our story. My hope is that it has inspired you to live your life in a greater capacity for generosity. You have the generosity gene. Activate it and live it out to its fullest potential. I can promise you that you will never regret it. Finally, I do not expect to see the greatest harvest of my life and ministry. But this one thing I know: I may never see it, but I will live it! You do the same!

Chapter 12 Takeaway

After reading the stories in this chapter, are you inspired to be generous even if your generosity goes unnoticed, unappreciated, or if you never get to see how it benefits others? Consider that seeing the harvest of your generosity is not a prerequisite to being generous.

Now that you have finished this book, how do you plan to activate your generosity gene? Perhaps take some time to meditate and pray about it. Has your plan changed over the course of reading *The Generosity Gene*? If so, how?

EPILOGUE

I mentioned in chapter 6 that Jamie was dealing with a serious health issue and that I hoped to provide an update once I reached the epilogue. Well, here we are, and I am pleased to say that after a challenging five months, there has been tremendous improvement in Jamie's health! It took a plethora of tests to finally get clarity and a successful treatment plan, but as I stated earlier, there continued to be a keen sense that we were waging a spiritual battle meant to disrupt the writing of this book. It's no coincidence that the completion of *The Generosity Gene* coincided with Jamie's improvement. We are truly grateful!

During the process of researching and simply trying to remember all the significant events in forty-plus years of marriage and ministry, something very unexpected transpired. As we began to rehearse each memory along our journey, we were able to relive each of the special moments shared in the pages of this book. This became such a rich experience for Jamie and me, one that we will cherish for the remainder of our days. Our hearts have overflowed with gratitude to the Lord for His faithfulness and blessings upon our life.

I want to close with a story we were reminded of during the process of writing, which epitomizes the message of *The Generosity Gene*.

As a youth pastor, I had taken and led multiple youth missions trips. I observed the difference these trips made in the lives of young people. When I became the lead pastor of a church in 1988, I continued leading missions trips that included the youth and adults. One of these trips was to Merida, Mexico. A lady named Janice participated in this trip, which included construction work, daily children's outreaches, and nightly services.

Janice approached me after the trip and shared how her life had been affected by this missions trip. The impact was so great that she made the decision to give everything above her living expenses toward missions. Janice faithfully continued to give all her expendable income for the next eleven years, at which time I left my pastorate and lost track of her and her ongoing missions commitment.

As I ponder Janice's incredible generosity journey, I believe she qualifies to be added to the list of nameless faith heroes mentioned in Hebrews 11. They are referred to as "others" or "they." On this side of heaven, most are unknown by the masses, and their stories are not widely shared. However, in heaven they *are* known! Like Janice and so many others, you may never end up seeing your greatest harvest on earth. Just know that it could be said about you: He/she never saw it; he/she lived it. Janice never saw it. She gave it!

PRAYER OF SALVATION

If you have never asked Jesus into your heart by praying a simple prayer of salvation, you can do so right now!

> Dear God, I know I am a sinner, and I ask for Your forgiveness. I believe Jesus Christ is Your Son. I believe that He died for my sins and that You raised Him to life. I want to trust Him as my Savior and follow Him as Lord from this day forward. Guide my life and help me to do Your will. I pray this in the name of Jesus. Amen!

Congratulations, you just made the most important decision of your life! Please let someone know that you prayed this prayer. If you do not have or know of a church to connect to, please contact us, and we will assist you.

ACKNOWLEDGEMENTS

I have so many people to thank for your love and support during both the writing of this book and my life in general.

First, I want to thank my mentor, spiritual father, and friend, Pastor Hugh Rosenberg. You have been one of the most significant influences in my life, especially in the area of generosity. Your story and life message are "Faith Promise Living." You modeled that the single greatest expenditure in our household budget should be missions. You did not just preach the message; you lived it. Jamie and I are indebted to you, Pastor Hugh, for ruining our life for the ordinary!

And then, our three daughters, Lindy, Kristy, and Keri. You have had a front-row seat to our story and have always cheered us on. We do what we do with our ministry, BJC Missions, because you gave us your blessing in November 2016. And you blessed us with the greatest blessings of all, our grandchildren, Ella, Brody, Hudson, and Easton!

To our family, friends, neighbors, mentors, churches, and ministry peers who have been instrumental in our journey over the past years. You have journeyed with us as we resigned from pastoral ministry, started a missions organization, completed a master's program, and wrote a book. Thank you for your love, support, and encouragement along the way. We are truly grateful for each of you!

Finally, a special thanks to the *Made For More* team: Jenna, Rigel, David, and Jill. Your tireless efforts in coaching, editing, cover design, publishing, and passion for excellence were of great value to me as I wrote *The Generosity Gene*!

Brian Campbell can be reached by visiting www.thegenerositygene.com

Made in the USA
Columbia, SC
11 February 2023

11988845R00111